TIBET

TIBET

The lost civilisation

Simon Normanton

VIKING

For all Tibetan children

VIKING

Published by the Penguin Group
Penguin Books Ltd, 27 Wrights Lane, London W8 5TZ
Viking Penguin Inc., 40 West 23rd Street, New York, New York 10010, USA
Penguin Books Australia Ltd, Ringwood, Victoria, Australia
Penguin Books Canada Ltd, 2801 John Street, Markham, Ontario, Canada L3R 1B4
Penguin Books (NZ) Ltd, 182-190 Wairau Road, Auckland 10, New Zealand

Penguin Books Ltd, Registered Offices: Harmondsworth, Middlesex, England

First American Edition
Published by Viking Penguin Inc., 1989

10 9 8 7 6 5 4 3 2 1

Printed in Italy

Library of Congress Catalog Card Number: 88-50526

ISBN 0-670-82511-5

CONTENTS

PREFACE

This book tells the story of the unveiling and subsequent destruction of the old Tibet. It is compiled almost entirely from the words and pictures of some of those very few outsiders who visited Lhasa in the first half of this century.

These are:

Hugh Richardson	1936–1950
Heinrich Harrer	1946–1950 & 1982
Dr. Shen Tsung-Lien	1944–1948
Freddy Spencer Chapman	1936
Dr. James Guthrie	1936 & 1946
Sir Basil Gould	1936 & 1940
Sir Charles Bell	1920
Edmund Candler and members of the Younghusband Mission to Lhasa	1904

Much of the interpretation of events in Tibet, as described in this book, is derived from Hugh Richardson's *Tibet and Its History*. Hugh Richardson was British Political Representative in Lhasa from 1936 until 1947, with a short break as First Secretary at the British Legation in Chungking. After the transfer of power in India he stayed on in Lhasa until 1950 as representative of the new Indian Government. Hugh Richardson thus spent longer in Lhasa than any other European in the last 200 years. He had first-hand experience of the last days of the old Tibet. Throughout this book there are innumerable paragraphs, sentences and phrases taken from his writing or from interviews with him. I should like to take this opportunity to express my thanks for his help. I must also thank Heinrich Harrer for his help and for letting me quote at such length from his *Seven Years in Tibet* which was my introduction to the

Peasant woman below a monastery in central Tibet

country. My thanks too to Tony Isaacs, sometime Executive Producer of the BBC 'World About Us' series, who, with his usual faith in the possibility of all things, commissioned two colour archival films on Tibet. I would also like to thank James Woodall, my editor at Hamish Hamilton, for his patience. Finally I must thank all those who have lent their pictures, the fees for which will go to a Tibetan Children's Charity in India.

ACKNOWLEDGEMENTS FOR PHOTOGRAPHS

17, 72, 73, 74, 80, Sir Charles Bell.

64, 65, 69, 76, 77, 79, 82, 87, 88, Sir Charles Bell, courtesy of the Pitt-Rivers Museum, Oxford.

124 top, 131 top, 135, 171, Brooke Dolan and Ilya Tolstoy, Courtesy The Academy of Natural Sciences of Philadelphia.

177, 180 bottom, Eastphoto.

179, 180 top, 181, ETV Ltd.

22, 28, 29, 35 top, 36, 37, 40 lower, 43, 44 top, National Army Museum, London.

14, 15, 33, 45, 51, 56, India Office Library.

182, 183, Roma Gelder.

31 top, 33 top, Peter Goude.

130, Sir Basil Gould.

2, 33 lower, 119, 129 lower, 144, 154, 154, 160, 161 top, 164 top right, 166, 167, 168, Dr. James Guthrie, courtesy Mrs. Joan Guthrie.

163 lower, 172, 173, 175, 187 top and middle right, Prof. Heinrich Harrer.

99 bottom, 102, 104, 107, 108 top and bottom, 113 bottom, Lt-General Sir Philip Neame V.C., courtesy Lady Neame.

191, Office of Tibet, London.

190 right, Akong Rimpoche.

1, 2, 20, 23, 24, 25, 27, 30, 31 lower, 34, 35, 36 top, 38, 40, 42, 46, 47, 48, 54, 55, 71, 73, 83, 91 left, 92, 95, 96, 97, 99 top, 100, 105 right, 106, 111, 114, 115, 116, 117, 118, 119 left, 120 top, 121 left, 126, 127, 128, 129 top, 133, 136, 140, 146, 147, 148 centre, 149 centre, 151, 153, 156 top, 159, 165, 170, 187 top left, 190 left, Hugh Richardson.

192, Leon Schadeberg

186, 187 bottom, Tedeus Scorupski.

122, 123, 124 lower, 137, 139, 142, 143, 145, 146 top left, 148 top, 149 top and bottom, 150, 151, 152, 155, 156 bottom, 157, 158, 161 bottom left, 162, 163 top, 164, 169, Dr. Tsung-lien Shen.

8, 70, 85, 120 lower, 131 lower, George Sherriff.

60 right, 68, 101, 103, 105 left, 108 centre, 110, 113, 121 right, 161 bottom right, F. Spencer Chapman.

174, Jigme Taring.

120, 185, Tenzin Tethong.

185, 188, Phuntsog Wangyal.

93, Frederick Williamson, courtesy Mrs. Margaret Williamson.

INTRODUCTION

Some years ago I was working in Nepal, making a film for the BBC. I was staying with a friend in Kathmandu. One evening, idly looking through the books on the shelves, I pulled out a tattered paperback. Perhaps it was 'Tibet' in its title that stirred my interest. From my bedroom window I could see the white peaks of the Himalayas. Beyond them lies Tibet. There is something alluring about that mysterious country.

The book was called *Seven Years in Tibet*, by Heinrich Harrer, an Austrian climber, who was interned by the British in India when the Second World War broke out. Together with a friend he escaped and crossed the Himalayas into Tibet.

Some time later, back in the office in London, I was telling a colleague, Christine Carter, about this Tibet I had read of; how it seemed to have been such a remarkable country; how it was said to have been completely destroyed by the Chinese; how I had never seen any film of that old Tibet.

Christine set about some detective work. She discovered who, in the first half of this century, had crossed the Himalayas to the forbidden city of Lhasa. It was a short list. Tibet then was out of bounds – remote, unvisited, a place almost nobody went to. We traced them, or their descendents, and found, hidden away in attics, forgotten reels of film and piles of old photographs. Much of the film and many of the photographs were in colour, dating from a time when colour was rare and expensive. From the films we made two programmes; 'Tibet, The Lost Mystery', which chronicles the unveiling of Tibet, and 'Tibet, The Bamboo Curtain Falls', relating the appalling desecration of Tibet after the Chinese takeover. Those programmes have now been shown in many countries around the world. Since then I have made two further documentaries. They vividly portray the ancient secular and religious ceremonies of Lhasa, and bear the title of this book, *Tibet, the Lost Civilisation*.

The old Tibet has gone forever. Little remains to tell of what it was like, save the memories, films and photographs of those few outsiders who were there. This book is compiled entirely from their words and pictures. It is a first-hand account by people who knew that old Tibet. All I have done is to piece together, from the books they wrote, a continuing story of which their various adapted accounts here constitute chapters; the story of the undoing of

9

Tibet. It is a unique record in colour of a lost civilisation that can never now be seen; but then, at the beginning of this century, there was no living European who had ever seen Lhasa. Shrouded by impenetrable secrecy on the roof of the world, it was said to be the one mystery that the 19th century had left to the 20th to explore.

AUTHOR'S NOTE

The majority of the colour photographs in this book were taken by amateurs with simple cameras between 1920 and 1949. These Lumiere Autochromes, Finlay-Pagets and Dufaycolours were pioneering colour processes. The manufacture of the film was complex and expensive. They needed relatively long exposure even in good light and that could cause a blurring of movement. Then they deteriorated quickly in adverse conditions; the starch base would grow mould spots in damp atmosphere, the colours fade in daylight. The rare examples on the following pages are remarkable not only for their good condition but for the fact that they are of Lhasa, the most exclusive, mysterious, unvisited city on earth. It is extraordinary that they should have remained unseen for so long. Together with some of the first Kodachromes and some enlargements from 16 millimetre colour film taken in the 1940s, these pictures give a unique view across almost half a century into a vanished world.

Simon Normanton
May 1988

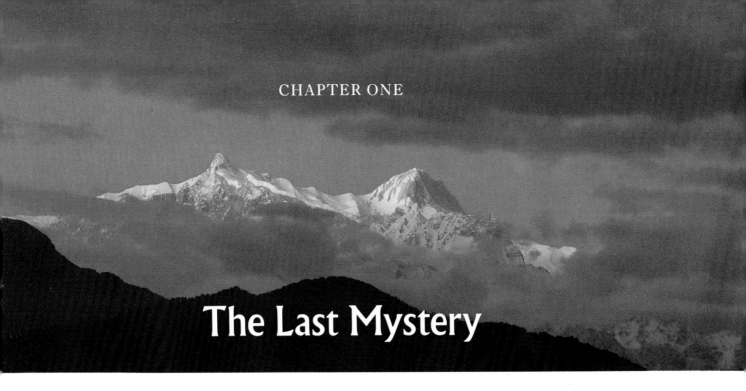

CHAPTER ONE

The Last Mystery

IT is the year 1900. You are travelling by train. For hours you have been crossing the swaying plains of Northern India, leaning against the window, the telegraph lines looping by; the air is hot and dusty, smelling of coal smoke from the engine; white-clad villagers are harvesting in a sea of fields and in the distance is the dim blue of the foothills, the home of tigers and hill-people, that merge into the clouds. Then you see them. It is a surprise for you realise they have been there all the while, high above the foothills; the Himalayas, a distant crest of snowpeaks already turning pink in the quickening afternoon.

The Himalayas mark the northern border of India, the natural frontier between the Indian subcontinent and Central Asia. They are the silent guardians of the high passes that lead into Tibet. Tibet is out of bounds, closed to all foreigners. High up, beyond the Himalayas, they say it is a vast tableland, silent and windswept, with occasional nomads and their black tents and scattered herds: and then, somewhere, there are monasteries full of murmuring lamas; finally, Lhasa, which, they say, means 'The Place of God'. Only one Englishman has ever been there, a moody eccentric called Thomas Manning, nearly 100 years ago.

In Manning's time, at the beginning of the last century, Lhasa was just another unexplored corner of the earth. The world was full of 'heathen tribes and exotic mumbo-jumbo'; there was all of darkest Africa, the lost cities of the Amazon, the buffalo-roaming Indians of America, let alone Central Asia. But now, at the beginning of the 20th century, things are very different. We have explored to the ends of the earth. Just this one country remains, unseen, unvisited, defying the most intrepid adventurers to enter her closed gates.

THE politics of Asia in 1900 were very different from those in Manning's time. British power and prestige now pressed against the southern borders of the Himalayas, the frontier of the Empire.

The goings-on north of that border were of no small concern to the government of India. The Russian Empire in Asia had been expanding eastward with a gathering and seemingly unstoppable momentum. This advance towards India was relentless and deeply disturbing. No one could view with equanimity this challenge to British prestige and influence. Conflict seemed inevitable. Already fear of Russian intentions had provoked two British invasions of Afghanistan. The North-West Frontier was a constant ferment of unruly tribes. In that, there was more than a little of Russia's hand.

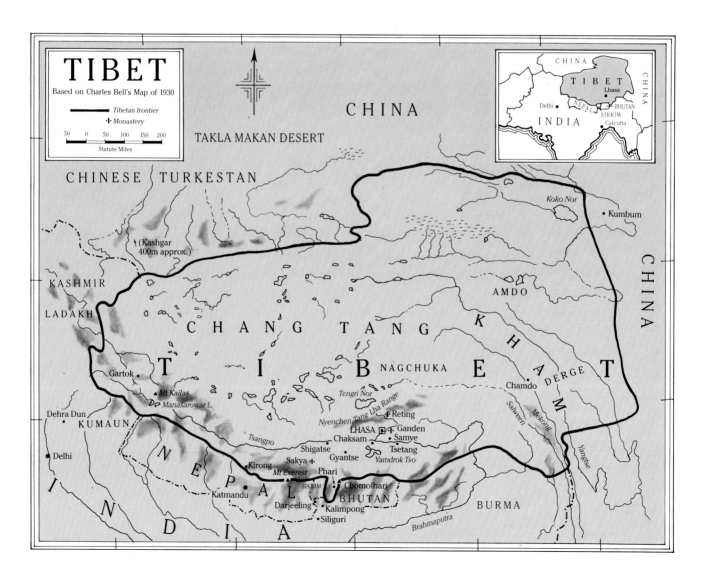

It was in the light of this Russian expansion in Asia that, at the turn of the century, the Government of India looked up at the frontier with Tibet and wondered just what intrigues the Russians were fomenting in that secretive hinterland. What if by some bold move the Russians were suddenly to establish themselves in Lhasa and thereby become a dominating and de-stabilising influence overlooking the plains of India?

There were rumours circulating in Calcutta of Russian dealings with Tibet. Russian agents were reported to have been in Lhasa. No one was in any doubt that something had to be done. Lord Curzon, the newly appointed Viceroy of India, was determined that relations with Tibet should be clarified. An effort should be made to enter into direct negotiations with the Lhasa Government. A letter was addressed to the Dalai Lama and after some difficulty a trader was found to convey it across the forbidden frontier to the heart of the mysterious kingdom.

As Lord Curzon and the officials, charged with the responsibility of governing India, anxiously awaited the reply at Government House in Calcutta before deciding what should be done about Tibet, they were not in total ignorance about the country.

The Tibetans' policy of excluding foreigners had, for many years, prompted a quest for information about the country. It came from a variety of sources; from the few westerners who trespassed beyond the frontier, mostly to remote and sparsely populated areas, from the trickle of traders and pilgrims which came down from Tibet, from border officials and missionaries in regions to the south of the Himalayas that had connections with Tibet of a religious or customary kind. In particular, information came from the determined explorations of the Pundits, specially trained native agents of the Survey of India. Disguised as pilgrims, these courageous spies, with compasses concealed in their prayerwheels and telling the paces on their rosaries, had furtively paced the length and breadth of Tibet. They disappeared beyond the Himalayas, like the early explorers across the Atlantic, out of all contact with the civilised world. Some were gone for years, to emerge with tales of being sold into slavery or of meetings with the Dalai Lama in the Potala Palace in Lhasa, tales that served more to stir the popular imagination than to sate it. But the Pundits' brief was primarily concerned with the geography of Tibet, the distance between towns, the origin of certain rivers. From their reports and from the information gleaned from other sources a general picture of Tibet could be pieced together.

AS much as any country can be, Tibet is shut off from the rest of the world. Those who would approach from the south or west must push their way up through the great wall of the Himalayas, the highest mountain range in the world. To the north still more severe are the Arctic wastes of the Chang-Tang, the Northern Plains. Scoured by the wind and cracked by frost, this desolate region of tangled valleys and uplands, hundreds of miles across, and 1,000 miles in length, freezes out the strangers from more hospitable lands. Far to the east tumbled mountain ranges and the deep gorges of some of the worlds largest rivers, the Yangtse, the Mekong, the Salween, fence off the lowlands of China. Marco Polo in all his Asian wanderings never penetrated to Tibet. Neither did the Mongols, for all their far-ranging conquests, find any way through.

Within these natural defences Tibet is a high, cold country, more than ten times the size of Britain; half a million square miles of windswept steppes, most above 10,000 feet, much above 16,000. It is a dry country, comparatively infertile and sparsely populated. On the fringes of the Chang-Tang, scattered nomads drift with their flocks across distant, treeless plains and broad, stony valleys ringed by mountains. Brigands prey upon unprotected travellers.

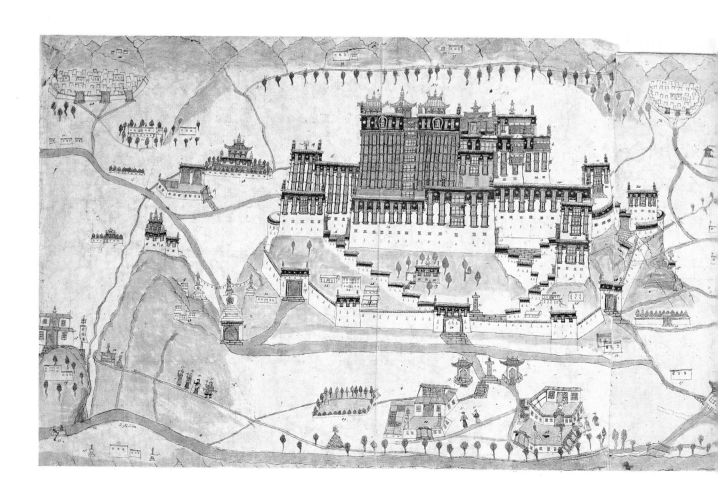

Early explorers, Dr. William Moorcroft
and Captain Hyder Jung Hearsey,
crossing the Himalayas into Tibet
towards Mount Kailas, 1812

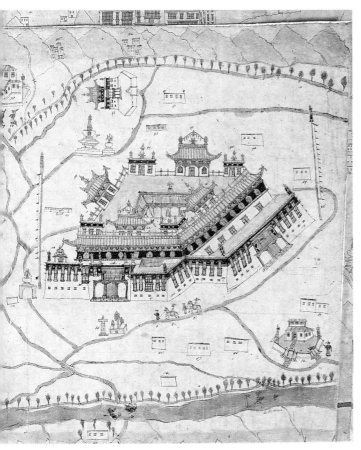

A drawing of Lhasa, circa 1859,
by a Tibetan lama, showing the Potala
and, to its right, the Jo-Khang

To the south of the Chang-Tang, south of the mountains the Tibetans call the Nyen Chen Tangh La, 'The Spirit of the Expanse of Great Fear', is the province of U, Central Tibet. Here, there are towns and villages. Monasteries are dotted over the mountainsides. Red-robed Buddhist monks go from village to village, intoning prayers and collecting alms. In this area converge trade routes, from China and India, from Mongolia and Turkestan and Siberia; for here is Lhasa, 'The Place of God', the Holy City. In Lhasa, the spiritual hub of Tibet, the God-King, the Dalai Lama, incarnation of Chenrezi, the Buddhist God of Mercy, rules from his Potala Palace.

The Tibetans have their own distinct customs and language. They belong to what is loosely called the Tartar branch of the human race. The majority are related in physical type to the people of the steppes and deserts further north. They are very different from the Indians to the south and easily distinguished from the Chinese to whom they are not closely related. They are more closely related to the Mongols. Like the Mongols they were once a restless, marauding people. In the 7th century Tibetan armies consolidated all of what is now Tibet. They imposed their authority far west to Kashmir, south into Nepal and India and upper Burma; they also invaded China.

The Emperor of China was forced to yield a princess in marriage to the conqueror, the young King of Tibet, who also took to wife a princess from Nepal. The two queens, being Buddhist, converted the King to their faith. He then used all his influence to spread Buddhism in Tibet. Over the ensuing centuries Buddhism prospered and the Tibetans turned themselves wholeheartedly to their religion. Monasteries were built and peopled with thousands of monks. The Emperor of China received Tibetan lamas at his court. Tibet in turn accepted the protection of China. It has always been a vague relationship, peculiarly oriental, namely that of two equals; Priest and Patron.

At the beginning of the 20th century, Tibet is nominally a remote corner of the Celestial Empire. But the Chinese can do nothing to protect Tibet. Lhasa is some 13 months distant from Peking; there are Chinese representatives there, Ambans, with vague influence in the governance of the country but the Emperor can claim little real authority in Lhasa.

For China, Tibet is a barrier to encroaching western influence. The Chinese connive at Tibet's isolation. The Tibetans have long since shut themselves off from the outside world. It is, above all, their sacred religion that they wish to protect from the predatory world that surrounds them – their religion and their fragile independence.

This, then, is Tibet, isolated between two converging powers, a vast empty square on the board of the great game.

Dorjieff

AS regards Tibetan thought, politics and way of life, the government of India was in almost total ignorance. Any information that the Pundits had gathered about Tibetan policy and political thinking was circumstantial, limited by their need to travel in disguise amongst the poorer people. They could provide little insight into the minds and customs of these obscure people.

After six months, Lord Curzon's letter to the Dalai Lama was returned; no one had dared deliver it. Another letter was sent. Some months later it too was returned, unopened.

By this time the Russian scare had become acute. There was no doubt that Russian agents had been in Lhasa. The British minister in St. Petersburg reported that a Tibetan monk named Dorjieff, an emissary from the Dalai

Lama, was known to have met with the Czar and delivered a letter. There were rumours in Peking about a secret agreement between Russia and China, assigning to Russia all Chinese interest in Tibet in exchange for Russia's support in maintaining the integrity of the Chinese Empire. Details of the proposed treaty were even published in the *China Times*.

Lord Curzon advocated a forward policy. A bold move might thwart the Russians. Whitehall was uneasy about any imperial adventures beyond the Himalayas but Curzon got his way. A small mission was permitted to advance just across the frontier into Tibet in an attempt to prompt the Lhasa Government to enter into negotiations. For five fruitless months the Tibetans all but ignored it. The mission would lose face by going back. Reluctantly, Whitehall conceded that a larger military force should be provided to escort the mission deeper into Tibet in the hope of bringing greater pressure to bear on the Tibetans. The mission was to be led by Colonel Younghusband, the escort commanded by General MacDonald.

It was 1904, the Tibetan Year of the Wood Dragon.

SOURCES

The paragraphs describing the history and geography of Tibet are derived from Charles Bell's book, *Portrait of the Thirteenth Dalai Lama*. My thanks to Wisdom Press for permission to quote from it. Some paragraphs are taken from the three other books Charles Bell wrote; *The People of Tibet*, *The History of Tibet* and *The Religion of Tibet*. Other sections, particularly the section on Pundits, are derived from Hugh Richardson's *Tibet and Its History*.

CHAPTER TWO

Across the Forbidden Frontier

The expedition assembled at Siliguri, the end of the plains railway at the foot of the Himalayas on the borders of Sikkim.

"UNITS forming the escort were coming in from all over India. Shrieking locomotives disgorged mountains of equipment. The railway station seethed with khaki-coloured military men amongst the piled-up stores, bullock carts, companies of marching men and a great army of coolies from all parts of the Himalayas.

"I met two major-generals who quite independently said that Tibet would be an 'A–1' place for curios. We were just like excited schoolboys. I must say, it really was rather fun, there's something so compelling about forbidden cities.

"The start-off from the scorching Indian plains, with their hot copper skies and roasted dust, for the cool hills is always exhilarating but this time it was especially so, bound as we were for the mystic land beyond the snows. We could see those snowy ranges from the plains, far away, towering high above the dark ramparts of the Himalayas. They glittered in the sunshine – cold, relentless and menacing, India's icy sentinels, over 20,000 feet above us.

"We were full of brains on that Lhasa column. There were men who had made the subject of Tibet their very own before they had ever set foot in the country. There was even a man with a bicycle wheel with which to correct all preconceived notions of Tibetan distances. There was a man with a butterfly net and another who collected stones and one with a trowel who collected weeds and a whole committee of licensed curio-hunters for the British Museum. Then there were the newspaper correspondents, devilish keen to be in on the show.

"It is a most impressive thing, an expeditionary force on the march. One is so apt to think of an army on a parade ground. Even so small a force as ours stretches for miles along the road. The dust crawls out slowly from under the changing feet of men and animals, and hangs in the air for a mile behind the last files of the rearguard.

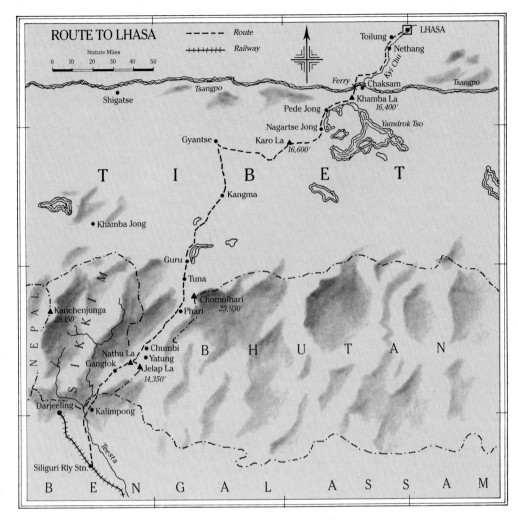

"Two days' marching took us out of India into Sikkim but we were in the heart of the jungle almost as soon as we left Siliguri. Even for troops marching along the road it has a certain fascination; the incessant call of the jungle fowl, the constant shade so unusual in India, the steamy hothouse atmosphere, gorgeous butterflies and bright orchids in the treetops. On the road we passed traders coming down from Tibet, accompanied by huge mastiffs and leading shaggy ponies laden with wool that they had somehow managed to smuggle across the Himalayas despite the trade restrictions. They were picturesquely dressed, particularly their women folk in woollen kneeboots of red and green patterns, long russet cloaks, bound tightly at the waist and bulging out with cooking implements, and embroidered caps of every description. They were bright and good humoured, and twirled prayerwheels as they walked.

"We ascended beside a river, along a mule track newly blasted by the sappers, towards the Jelap-La, the pass which leads into Tibet.

"Within a few miles, puffing and panting up this stupendous winding staircase of the Himalayas, we passed from scorching midsummer into midwinter, from semi-tropical jungle to broken rock and shale and frozen snow. The pass is at 14,390 feet. On first aquaintance, such an altitude impresses one greatly. There is something so strange about the atmosphere that one feels as though one were on another planet.

"The mountains were strangely silent. The only sound was of mountain choughs which flew round and round in an unsettled manner, whistling querulously as though in complaint at the intrusion of their solitude.

"The pass was marked by a row of cairns from which fluttered prayerflags and tattered bits of votive raiment. On gaining the summit we found it swept

by an icy blast which snatched away our breath and pierced our thickest garments. This made it impossible to stand at the top for more than an instant. In that instant we caught a glimpse of a sea of wild hilltops, dashed here and there with snow. From our feet a stony track sank down into a deep ravine of dark pine trees, and a valley far below us. In the far distance was the white speck of a monastery. Here then was Tibet, the forbidden, the mysterious.

"We slipped and slithered down the loose shoot of frost-splintered rocks which formed the track, out of the wind, to the shelter of the pines 2,000 feet below. Dark began to fall. A procession appeared coming up the valley escorting some Chinese mandarins, a reminder that we had trespassed into a remote corner of the Celestial Empire. With them was the Tibetan governor of the valley. They each had a huge umbrella of honour carried over them. Having heard of our advance, they had come to tell Colonel Younghusband to go back. They were told that that was now impossible, whereupon they quietly disappeared down the glen into the darkness.

"The next morning, we were all up and off by daybreak. That first valley in Tibet was charming. There were grassy meadows and woods dotted with fine large houses in the Swiss chalet style, with widely projecting eaves and wooden balconies carved and gaudily painted.

"Crowds of excited inhabitants, including many red-robed monks, stood by the roadside staring in open-mouthed astonishment at our invasion of their valley.

"The Tibetan governor, a big, lusty, well-bred, youngish man, came again with the Chinese officers and urged Younghusband to remain here for two or three weeks until he could write to Lhasa and get a reply from the Dalai Lama. The commissioner insisted it was impossible to discuss matters here or with anyone but the proper representatives from Lhasa. The governor was crestfallen. Immediately after lunch he disappeared back up the valley to his fort at a place called Phari.

"We continued our advance. The valley, as we got higher, became very bold and wild. The trees thinned and disappeared at 13,350 feet. We then emerged from the rugged ravines onto the open, bare, windswept plateau of

Tibet. The huge white mass of Mount Chomolari, 'The Mountain Goddess of the Snows', rose, awe-inspiring, above the plain. It was bitterly cold, beyond belief. The poor chilled troops and followers huddled together in their tents for warmth and kept up a chorus of coughs and sneezes through the sleepless night.

"Across the plain stood the great fort of Phari, like a medieval castle in Europe. As we approached the town we could see that there was a great commotion. The people were buzzing about like bees. A deputation came out to beg General Macdonald not to enter the town or fort. The general assured them there was nothing to fear as long as they remained friendly.

"The town of Phari consists of about 200 mean, low-roofed, windowless huts, built of black peat-sods and huddled round the fort. The town is appallingly foul and dirty. The majority of the population of about 2,000 were women, equally dirty. Perhaps this does to some extent protect them against the cold on this most miserable spot of the earth. Both men and women cover themselves with jewellery. The married women wear a most curious hooplike headdress ornamented with turquoises and ruby-coloured stones.

"In the fort the first thing one saw of a morning were these grimy sirens, climbing the stairs, burdened with buckets of chopped ice and sacks of yak dung, the two necessaries of life.

"The Tibetan coolie women are merry folk. They laugh and chatter at their work all day long and do not in the least resist the familiarities of the Gurkha soldiers. Sometimes, as they pass one, they giggle coyly and put out their tongues, which is the Tibetan way of showing respect to those in high places. Their merriment sounds unnatural in all this filth and cold and squalor. After a week in Phari one quite forgot the mystery of Tibet."

"We sat out the winter in rain, wind and sleet on the grey desolate plain round Phari and the village of Tuna, a few deserted houses some miles further on. It was quite evident that our occupation had not in the least influenced the Lhasa monks toward making any effort for a settlement.

"The severity of the Tibetan winter began to abate with the opening of the Tibetan New Year, which coincides more nearly than our own with the natural division of the calendar. This year it fell in the middle of February. It was an occasion of great celebration amongst the villagers, with drinking and singing and all of them dressed in their best. A number of nomadic herdsmen came to the fairs. Their large black tents of woven yak hair accommodate 20 or 30 people, their boxes arranged around the inside. In the centre of the tent always stands a small shrine with some images.

'. . . the great fort of Phari'

On the high plateau of Tibet

The Tuna plain

Chomolhari above Tuna

"We were at last ordered to advance deeper into the forbidden land. As we marched out of Phari there was a feeling of exhilaration amongst the troops. It was a brilliant sunny day. The housetops of the town were crowded with excited Tibetans.

"The Lhasa general and his retinue arrived. They spread a rug on the ground and sat down in a ring in the middle of the plain to discuss the situation. They reiterated their old demand; 'Go back to Yatung, then we will negotiate.' (Yatung is a village on the border.) 'Tell them,' Colonel Younghusband said to the interpreter, 'we have been trying to negotiate with Tibet for 15 fruitless years. We have been in Phari for three months waiting to meet responsible officials from Lhasa. We are now going on. We have no wish to fight and he would be well advised to order his soldiers to retire.'

"The Lhasa general was extremely perturbed. He got up and excitedly galloped off with his companions. He was a man of fine presence. One could not help but have sympathy for his predicament. His orders were to oppose our advance but to avoid a battle; ours to avoid a battle but to continue our advance.

"The Tibetans had built a wall right across our line of march. We went right up to the wall and started to wrest their muskets from them. It was ridiculous, the outcome inevitable. A shot was fired, whereupon all hell broke loose in an explosion of shooting. Then the Tibetans just bowed their heads and turned and walked away, as if they were disillusioned with their gods. Why in the name of all their Buddhas didn't they run?

"They opposed us all the way to Gyantse. They were mostly impressed peasants. Never was there such hopeless and ineffectual gallantry.

"We buried their dead where they lay but the Tibetans came in the night and dug them up again. It is their custom to leave their dead to the elements. The Tibetan wounded were brought into the camp. They showed extraordinary hardihood and stoicism. They were consistently cheerful and always ready to appreciate a joke. One man, who'd lost both legs, said: 'In my next battle I must be a hero for I cannot run away.' They never hesitated to undergo operations, did not flinch at pain and took chloroform without fear. Their recuperative power was marvellous. They became quite popular in camp, these wild, long-haired giants. They were so good-humoured and gentle in manner.

'They spread a rug on the ground and sat down in the middle of the plain.'   'The Tibetan wounded . . .'

◀ 'The Tibetans had built a wall
right across our line of march.'   'They became quite popular in camp.'

29

"We crossed another pass at 16,000 feet, which the Tibetans contested, before entering the broad valley of Gyantse. Here our eyes rid us of the fallacy that Tibet is all a vast, treeless and barren country peopled by nomads. Here was a well-watered plain dotted over with neat, whitewashed farmhouses and villas clustering in groves of trees amongst well-cultivated fields.

"Gyantse enjoys all the advantages of the ideal Tibetan town. It has a commanding fort, the Jong, on an upstanding rock like Edinburgh Castle. Not far from the fort is a huge monastery swarming with monks and, high up on the cold mountains above the valley, one sees the cold, bleached walls of other monasteries, some of them perched on almost inaccessible cliffs, whence they look sternly down on the warmth and prosperity below. It is a busy and important town of about 1,000 houses, at the junction of the roads from India and Bhutan, Ladakh and Central Asia. Its extensive market is the third largest in Tibet and famous for its carpets and woollen cloth. Several Chinese and Nepalese traders live here.

"The town was full of people; men, women and children. They were perfectly friendly. The mighty rupee worked wonders. Within a few days people of the town and nearby villages came flocking in scores to our camp

'. . . the broad valley of Gyantse'

Gyantse

'The Jong, like Edinburgh castle . . .'   31   Gyantse monastery

with all kind of things for sale, laden on their backs or on strings of yaks and donkeys, so that quite a large bazaar was formed around our camp. Even the lamas came trudging in with bags of grain or sheaves of fodder, or sacred scrolls and books and images, and bargained them for cash. A free hospital was opened. In the fields the peasantry were ploughing and sowing peaceably.

"Unarmed officers wandered freely around Gyantse town and the monks from the monastery willingly conducted parties over the most sacred spots. Those first few days in Gyantse were peaceful but reports began to come in that, far from attempting to enter into negotiations, the Lhasa Government was levying an army in Kham, the wild, warlike area of Tibet to the east and that already men were camped nearby."

"For three months we waited in Gyantse. There was constant skirmishing. There was no word from Lhasa. Peace negotiations fell through, the Lhasa Government seemed chaotic and conveniently inaccessible, the Dalai Lama suitably impersonal. There appeared to be no hope of an end to the deadlock. If they would not come to us then we must go to them.

"The advance to Lhasa began on July 14. It would be hard to find an occasion on any expedition when, to the individual soldier, going on seemed to mean so much and staying behind so little; forbidden cities are so fascinating, and the idea of assisting in drawing aside a purdah so appeals to the imagination.

"From Gyantse we plunged on into the unknown towards Lhasa which, we had reason to believe, lay in some hidden valley 150 miles to the north, beyond the unexplored valley of the Tsang-po.

"We climbed up again to the treeless zone, over 15,000 feet. The villages beside the road were deserted save for old women and barking dogs.

Monks at a ceremony in Gyantse

Gyantse market

Officials at a festival in Gyantse

"The Tibetans had to be dislodged from the pass. Some of the fighting took place at 19,000 feet and this is probably the highest elevation at which an action has been fought in history. I was sorry for these Tibetans, their struggle was so hopeless. They were brave and simple, and none of us bore them the slightest vindictiveness.

"We kept the prisoners busy in our camp. They were always ready to help. When they had nothing to do they would sit down in a circle and discuss things resignedly; sometimes they would ask to go home, but we had no guarantee they would not fight us again.

"Our march crossed wild, romantic mountain country, along the fringes of a huge, blue lake, the haunt of myriad ducks and geese. Valleys of mystery and gloom, where no white man has ever trod, intersected the hills.

"At every point along our advance a cavalcade of Tibetan envoys, under red · umbrellas and riding gaily-caparisoned mules and led by servants in gorgeous liveries, came hurrying up. They would not yield a point and refused even to discuss terms unless we returned to Gyantse. Colonel Younghusband was a monument of patience and impassivity, like one of their own Buddhas. He insisted that the treaty must now be signed at Lhasa.

'. . . into the unknown towards Lhasa'

'. . . along the fringes of a huge blue lake'

'. . . wild romantic country'

34

'. . . valleys of mystery and gloom'

'Some of the fighting . . .'

"After ten days on the march we left the lake, ascended another pass and suddenly found ourselves looking down on the great river that has been guarded from European eyes for nearly a century, the Tsang-po, the upper Brahmaputra. It wound, far below us, through a valley covered with green and yellow cornfields. Beyond lay hills even more barren and verdureless than those we had crossed. To the north-east was the Kyi-Chu valley in which lay Lhasa, only 56 miles distant.

"It took a week to transport the entire force across the river in a quaint, old barge that our advance party had captured. We left the Tsang-po and entered the Kyi-Chu valley. The heat was almost tropical. The valley is fine and open, well-cultivated and very productive with numbers of snug-looking villages and residences surrounded with groves of trees. As we went on, it became wider and wider and more and more fertile.

"We caught up with the Tibetan envoys. They were in a terrible state at our advance. They had halted once more to argue with Colonel Younghusband about the wickedness and futility of our going to Lhasa.

The Tsang-po

'We entered the Kyi-Chu valley.'

'. . . in a quaint old barge'

'They were in a terrible state at our advance.'

Crossing the Tsang-po

37

"The crisis had now come; who was going to be the first living European to set eyes on the forbidden city of the Dalai Lama?

"It was about half-past one the following day that we caught our first glimpse of the Potala palace. We had outridden the column by some distance. A light blue haze settled over the far-distant mountains that ringed the plain. There was a smell of fresh spring earth, the rustle of a breeze in the barley, the sun merciless in a whitened sky. Then, as we rode on, it came. In the far distance, across and beyond these flat fields of barley, a grey pyramid disengaged itself from behind the outer point of a grey, concealing spur . . . Lhasa.

"There it was at last, the never-reached goal of so many weary wanderers, the home of all the occult mysticism that still remains on earth, the lightwaves of mirage dissolving the far outlines of the golden roofs and dimly seen white terraces, the great palace of the God-King – the Potala.

"We strained our eyes trying to catch through our glasses some glimpse of the city and all felt a thrill of excitement at actually being within sight of our goal. It is almost exactly 100 years since Thomas Manning, the only Englishman until today who ever saw Lhasa, preceded us.

"We made our way along the pebble-strewn road, past whitened houses lurking here and there under the shade of the poplars begirt with green and rustling barley. On all sides of the plain are the spurs of vast mountains, snowcapped even now in July, and between the spurs lurk villages and the monasteries of which we had heard so much. Through the centre of the plain meander the Kyi-Chu river and the road to the western gate of the Holy City.

It lies concealed behind the twin hills which stand as sentinels upon the plain. Lhasa is literally hidden as if nature conspires in its seclusion."

"We halted for the night about seven miles from Lhasa. Long before the camp was settled a great deputation arrived from the city, abbots and lamas and lay officials in a great variety of brilliant coloured costumes and a fantastic variety of peculiarly shaped headgear. There were fluffy, yellow tam-o'-shanters, large, deep-fringed, circular bonnets like pink, silk lampshades, coal scuttles, flat crowns of claret-coloured velvet with long, bushy, crimson tassels. Those worn by the cupbearers to the abbots were like large waterjugs.

"They were more conciliatory and shook hands all round. There were the usual arguments, the usual prayers. They again asked that we should not enter Lhasa, the guardian hills of which were now clearly visible to the east. It was the same old game but the treaty was now to be signed in Lhasa and not one mile short of it. As the afternoon wore on the fruitless durbar slowly dissolved but not until the leading men had thoroughly satisfied the curiosity which almost every article of our dress and equipment excited.

"Personally I amused myself by showing them several illustrated weekly papers. It was curious to note that they did not seem at all impressed by the large portraits of beautiful and partly unclad ladies, which constituted no small part of the attractions of most of the periodicals we had with us."

"So ended the last day of our weary march from India. Tomorrow an epoch in the world's history will be marked. There will be no more forbidden cities, no unknown land. Tomorrow, when we enter Lhasa, we will have unveiled the last mystery of the East."

'The great monastery of Drepung . . .'

CHAPTER THREE

The Unveiling of Lhasa

"FULL of anticipation, we started off the next morning. The scenery was most romantic, the valley fertile and picturesque, the hillsides rising into rugged pinnacles. The weather cleared up and became bright and sunny. The great monastery of Drepung, the largest in the world, stood up proudly under the foot of the hills. Its golden roofs glinted in the sunshine above tier upon tier of white buildings, the dormitories and chapels of nearly 8,000 monks. It looked like a town on the Riviera.

"Crowds of lamas were coming and going to Lhasa, some riding on ponies. The inhabitants paid no attention to us and continued their usual occupations as if the appearance of a foreign force was an everyday occurrence.

"To catch a glimpse of the sacred city several of us hurried on. It must be the most hidden city on earth. A huge rock on which stands the Chagpori, the medical college, rises bluffly from the river bank. Between it and the Potala hill is a ridge that screens the town from sight. Through a narrow gap, over which stands a typical Tibetan shrine, is the main gateway into Lhasa. It was crowded with inquisitive monks and townspeople.

"We dismounted and ascended the ridge towards the Chagpori. From here a breathtaking panorama of the Holy City, the Rome of Central Asia, was suddenly exposed to view. In front of the Potala, which soared skyward on our left, was a mile-wide belt of glades and woodlands over and between which the city of Lhasa peeps, an adobe stretch of flat-topped houses crowned with a blaze of golden roofs, the temples and palaces of the long-sealed, forbidden city. The mystery which had so long haunted our dreams lay revealed before our eyes at last. But a man can have no eye for anything but the vast mass of the Potala, the palace-temple of the Dalai Lama. White-buttressing curtains of stone, each a wilderness of close-ranked windows, reared up towards the sky. It was a sight full worthy of all the rumour and romance with which it had been invested for so many years. Little wonder that the Tibetans wished to keep their chief city secluded from the prying, curious world.

"The camp was by this time pitched on the plain behind the Potala."

'. . . the palace-temple of the Dalai Lama'   42

"TODAY, August 4 1904, we entered Lhasa to visit the Chinese Amban. We found the city almost deserted. It is squalid and filthy beyond description, undrained and unpaved, the streets after rain being nothing but pools of stagnant water, frequented by pigs and dogs searching for refuse. The city is generally smaller than we had anticipated, barely half a mile square, its streets rather narrow. There are no pavements as there is no wheeled traffic. The houses are substantially built with stone walls two or three storeys high, carefully whitewashed and generally with shops in the lower storey. They have flat roofs and the beams of the eaves are elaborately painted in red, blue and brown. A religious look is given to the streets by the tall prayer flags at the chief corners and numerous little incense kilns beside the doors of the houses.

"The Amban received the mission with elaborate ceremony. His Excellency is a middle-aged man of pleasing manners. It is quite possible that he

'August 4, 1904 . . .'

Inside the gateway

'We returned through the heart of the city.'

44

'. . . the front of the Jo-Khang cathedral' ▶

was sincere in his desire to effect a settlement. He contemptuously referred to the Tibetans as ignorant, blustering savages and deplored their dark cunning which, he naively remarked to the commissioner, 'you and I would never think of practising.' The Amban seemed more preoccupied with the precariousness of his own position than anything else. His memory dwelt somewhat persistently upon the assassinations that had overtaken two of his predecessors in office.

"We returned to camp through the heart of the city, followed everywhere by the eyes of a sullen crowd of lamas and laity which filled the sidestreets and the doorways, windows and roofs of the houses along the line of march. Many of them bolted to get a second look at us at a point further along. Most of the nobles and abbots, and the majority of the better class people, had fled the city.

"We were diverted from passing the actual front of the Jo-Khang cathedral, the great central temple of Lhasa, but were able to get a first glimpse of its timbered and painted portico and hanging draperies. A crowd of villainous-looking monks were gathered sullenly before the great barred doors. And

above all this loomed the Potala. There was no one who did not look up from time to time at that frowning cliff of a thousand sightless windows. It captured and held the imagination. One wondered what was going on behind the blind walls and imagined the lamas invoking the aid of their Gods to overthrow the intruders who had destroyed the inviolability of their sacred place.

"But the Dalai Lama had achieved the impossible. The God-King had disappeared, vanished, been spirited into the air, borne away by night in his palanquin no one knows whither or when. One imagined the awed attendants, the burying of treasure, the locking and sealing of chests, faint lights flickering in the passageways, hurried footsteps in the corridors, then the procession by moonlight up the valley to the north where the roar of the stream would drown the footsteps of the palanquin-bearers. The flight was really secret; it added fearfully to the mystery of the place."

"In the afternoon we were visited by a large body of Tibetan officials. They did not consider themselves in the least degree conquered nor were they at all inclined to make a treaty.

'. . . marshes where wild ducks flaunt their security'   46

"Colonel Younghusband puts the question direct to a head lama; 'Have you any news of the Dalai Lama? Do you know where he is?' The man looks slowly to the left and right and answers, 'I know nothing.' 'The ruler of your country leaves his palace and capital and you know nothing?' 'Nothing,' answers the monk, shuffling his feet but without changing colour.

"Nothing in the way of a settlement could be arrived at."

"During the protracted negotiations, we could visit the town fairly freely. The environs are beautiful with willowed groves intersected by clear-running streams, walled-in parks with palaces and fishponds and marshes where wild ducks flaunt their security. Ripe barley fields stretch away to the hills. A circular road, the Lingkor, the Holy Walk, winds round Lhasa. Pilgrims and devotees walk slowly around it, whirling their prayerwheels and mumbling charms and always keeping the Potala on their right."

"In the town the streets are thronged. In the bazaar, in the great square surrounding the cathedral, there is a bright and interesting crowd, as good-

47

Rock paintings on the Lingkhor, below the medical college

natured as you might meet anywhere; shiny-pated, ruby-coloured monks, bejewelled townswomen in all their silks and finery, travel-stained nomads, pilgrims from Mongolia and the Russian steppes, ruddy-cheeked men in greasy sheepskins astride unkempt ponies. Their fair-complexioned women, also mounted, are covered in bright silver and brass trinkets stuck over their dresses and tied to the long plaits of their hair. Their valuables are laden on shaggy, double-humped Bactrian dromedaries with collarbells tinkling in the confined and crowded thoroughfares. In the crowd you see white-turbaned Mohammedan merchants from Ladakh, Kashmir and Tartary, swarthy crop-haired, kilted Bhutanese, fairer Nepalese and quaintly-garbed countryfolk from distant provinces. All, however wild, reflect the religious atmosphere of the city by twirling their prayerwheels or counting their rosary beads even while chatting and trading.

"Among the crowds are officers and men; Tommies, Gurkhas, Sikhs and Pathans, stared at and criticised good-humouredly, their accoutrements fingered and examined. In a corner of the square a streetsinger with a guitar and dancing children attracts a small crowd. The crowd is parted by a government official riding past in bright yellow silks, followed by a mounted retinue in eccentric headgear.

"On fine days the wares are spread out on stalls and on the cobbles of the street; coloured cloths, trinkets, eatables, drugs and books, a pretty show against the dazzling, whitewashed exteriors brightened by caged, singing birds, larks, rosefinches and doves, and on the windowsills pots of flowers. The interiors of the houses look dark and disgustingly dirty. British officers haunt the bazaars looking for curios, but with very little success. Most of the knickknacks come from India and China. We found two quart bottles of Bulldog stout. It was in good frothy condition. In the purlieus of the city we found a bicycle without tyres and a sausage machine made in Birmingham.

"In the town, which has a population of about 10,000, women vastly outnumber men. The preponderance is perhaps due to the enormous quantity of men who become celibate monks and live in the surrounding monasteries.

"Tibet is really ruled by religion. There are three great monasteries outside the town, Drepung with 8,000 monks, Sera with 7,000 and then, 25 miles outside, Ganden with 5,000. There are other smaller monasteries in Lhasa. In the centre of the town is the Jo-Khang, the sacred heart not just of the Holy City but of Central Asia. From outside it is not at all imposing, high blank walls and a forest of dingy pillars beside a massive door.

"The door, thrown open, reveals a huge cloistered courtyard with pillars and Buddhist paintings on the walls, masses of hollyhocks, marigolds,

Ganden

Sera

49

nasturtiums and stocks in the centre and storerooms around the sides. On the upper floor the monks have their cells. Looking up there are hundreds of them gazing down at us over the banisters.

"The great doorway swings shut behind us."

"We enter the main temple by a dark passage. A service is being held as we enter. There is a thunderous harmony like an organ peal, a clashing of cymbals, a beating of drums and a blowing of trumpets and conch shells. Then the music dies away like the reverberation of cannon in the hills. The temple would be dark if it were not for the flickering of thousands of candles and butterlamps, row upon row of them, placed before every shrine. The abbot seated in the centre begins the chant and the 1,000 monks, sitting cross-legged facing each other in rows, repeat the litany. They have extraordinarily deep and impressive voices. It is like the drone of some subterranean monster. The monks sway rhythmically as they endlessly repeat the formula.

"To visit the chief shrine our guide lights a torch and leads us through dark, covered passages lined by rows of images. Passages lead off to side chapels full of idols and relics in front of which buttercandles flicker. Half-seen figures people the recesses and line the sides of the paths along which we grope our way. The floor is slippery, worn down by centuries of pious feet.

"The air is heavy with the acrid reek of burning butter. Ten paces more and the great glowing mass of the Jo, the most famous idol in the world, looms out gleaming dull gold, shadowless and ghostlike in the tender glow of rows of butterlamps. It is uncannily impressive. The features of the young Buddha are smooth, almost childlike. No doubt the surroundings account for much of

the effect but as one gazes one knows that this most beautiful statue is the sum and climax of Tibet and one respects the jealousy of its guardians."

"This is the image that was brought from Peking over 1,200 years ago, part of the dowry of one of the wives of King Son-sen-gampo who, in the days when the Tibetans were a warrior race, had conquered China. It was he who built the Jo-Khang and established Buddhism in Tibet."

"In another room, on the floor above, was a fearful image of the dreaded Palden Llhamo, the goddess of disease, battle and death. It was quite overrun with little white mice that scurried unmolested over the floor, feeding on the cake and grain offerings, under the altar and up and down the bodies of the monks who were chanting her litany. The mice were said to be reincarnated monks and nuns. The effigy was surrounded by a vast collection of very ancient arms and armour. The lamas could not be induced to part with any of it, at any price.

"In the porch we found a large bell, on which were inscribed the words *Te Deum Laudamus*. It must have been a relic of an old Catholic mission that had been in Lhasa some 250 years before.

"As we emerged from the dark enclosures of the Jo-Khang into blazing sunlight we found half the population of Lhasa in a dense, growling crowd. The first stone missed us by inches. It signalled a score of others. They were obviously directed at our Chinese escort rather than ourselves. We rode out slowly, trying to look as dignified as we could. This spontaneous and popular outburst indicated the utter contempt felt by the Tibetans for the Chinese who had put up a proclamation deposing the vanished Dalai Lama. It was defaced by the populace."

"One could not help dwelling on the flight of the Dalai Lama. The Nepalese resident, a podgy little man, very ugly and good-natured with a face generally expanded in a broad grin, shook with laughter when we asked him if he knew the God-King. It was very funny, the idea of this irreverent little man hobnobbing with the divine.

"'I have seen him,' he said and exploded again.

"'But what does he do all day?' we asked.

"The resident puckered his brow, aping abstraction, and began to wave his hand in the air solemnly, with a slow circular movement, mumbling to the revolution of an imaginary prayerwheel. He was immensely pleased with the effect it produced on a sepoy orderly.

"Asking questions here is fruitless; one can learn nothing in this city of evasiveness."

"The political deadlock continued for weeks. The replies to our demands were an epitomé of Tibetan national character. The indemnity, they said, ought to be paid by us and not by them. We had invaded their territory and should bear the cost. Instead of discussing matters vital to the settlement, the Tibetans would arrive with all formality and ceremonial and then beg us not to cut the grass in a particular meadow or request the return of some empty grain bags to a monastery. It was most trying.

"We visited all the monasteries around Lhasa, either on private visits or when foraging for supplies. The small monasteries cling to the tops of hillsides, as if left behind in some great flood, with a few vacant monks. The larger monasteries are rather like our universities, Oxford and Cambridge, huge collections of temples and monastic buildings, larger and more inspiring

'. . . their unwilling contribution'

than most towns in Tibet. They maintain a dominating influence in Lhasa. In Drepung there are four colleges, one with mostly Mongolian monks. (Dorjieff was a Drepung monk.) Drepung was particularly obstructive and failed to carry out its promise to supply grain which we were to pay for generously.

"Imagine their consternation when an officer with an armed escort rode up to the gate with a letter saying that if the provisions were not handed over we would shell the monastery. The messengers were met by a crowd of excited lamas who refused to accept the letter, waved them away and rolled stones towards them menacingly.

"We moved the guns up.

"Groups of monks came out with a white flag, carrying gifts of baskets of eggs and a white scarf. They bowed and chattered and protested, and condescended to talk the matter over if we went away.

"We moved the guns up closer, deployed the infantry, and sat and watched, and smoked our pipes and waited.

"One had to have some sympathy for the Tibetans. They are civilised, if medieval, feudal even. The monks are the overlords, the peasantry their serfs. But the poor are not oppressed or discontented, though they give more than a tithe of their small income to the Church. It must be remembered that every family contributes at least one member to the priesthood. The laymen are not the victims of the monasteries so much as the servants of a community chosen from amongst themselves, and with whom they are connected by family ties.

"At last a thin line of monks, each carrying a bag of supplies, was seen to issue from the gate and descend the hill, a procession of sullen ecclesiastics who had never bowed or submitted to external influences in their lives, carrying on their backs their unwilling contribution to the support of the first foreign army that had ever intruded on their seclusion. The crisis was over.

"Throughout this rather trying time our social relations with the Tibetans were of a thoroughly friendly character. The Shap-pes, (the Cabinet Ministers), and one or two of the leading monks attended the race-meetings and gymkhanas that were got up to pass the time. They put their money on the tote and seemed to enjoy the day out. When their ponies ran in the visitors' race, they were genuinely excited. They were entertained to lunch and tea by Colonel Younghusband, and on these occasions they were genial and friendly. The humbler people showed no sign of resenting our presence in the city.

"Shooting was prohibited for fear of offending the Lamas by the taking of life. Much of our time we spent on rambles in the country round Lhasa, through gardens and orchards that supply the markets with vegetables and fruits, across parks, to the fields and shaggy stretches of woodland. The banks of the numerous streams are a mass of wild flowers. Up the valley the fields of ripening corn seem to stretch like a sea for miles. In the Dalai Lama's fields below the Potala, harvesters have commenced work, singing light-heartedly, the women wearing yellow garlands of wild clematis. A few fields are being ploughed with primitive wooden ploughs. Beside the comfortable farmhouses cattle are grazing, and under the shade of a clump of old willows ponies are sheltering from the sun and the flies.

"The villas and farmhouses are built round a central courtyard, the cattle stalled underneath, together with the stores and in the upper storey, fronted with a balcony and open verandah, are the human dwellings and cooking rooms. Windows are conspicuously few and small, so as to keep out the winter wind and cold. There are no chimneys but only a hole in the roof, so everything in the interior is more or less tanned by the smoke. Most of the gardens grow excellent potatoes.

"The chief amusements of the men seem to be horse-racing, wrestling, archery, dominoes and a game like draughts called 'pushing the tiger'. They are fond of dancing and singing, accompanied by the guitar, flute or bell. Children fly paper kites. Theatrical performances seem very popular and are held in the open air in a street or courtyard. They are given on the occasion of a festival, the general public being admitted free, at the expense of some well-to-do person. Though religious there is always a large element of buffoonery. They last for several hours each day and the spectators bring some work with them, mending or spinning. Both poor and well-to-do are much given to picnicing under the trees, with their families and dogs. We passed several such groups.

"Eventually on September 7, the treaty was signed with great pomp and ceremony in the Dalai Lama's throne room in the Potala. Our troops lined the road all the way from the foot of the hill up to the great gate of the venerable palace which looked down grimly on the grand display. The mission and military escort rode in procession, dismounted and climbed up steps. We passed along a maze of slippery passages, dimly illuminated by flickering butterlamps held by aged monks, impassive and inscrutable, to the throne room itself. The scene was very picturesque and impressive; a colourful crowd of councillors and tightly-packed British officers against the brilliant-hued background of frescoes on the walls and the bright mosaics of the beams and surrounding balconies.

"The essence of the agreement was that the Tibetans should have no dealings with any foreign government (really meaning the Russians) without first consulting us. Then there were other clauses, about the opening up of trade and the establishing of a trade agency, about respecting the frontiers between India and Tibet, and about an indemnity to be paid by the Tibetans. The seal of the Dalai Lama was affixed by the senior lama present. The lamas showed no sign of displeasure as they added their names.

"The Chinese did not sign. It was apparent to everyone that the Chinese had no real authority and that the Tibetans did not accept Chinese dictates in their internal affairs. The Amban was sitting on a smouldering volcano. He had been recruiting extra bodyguards in anticipation of our departure.

"There was much self-congratulation and celebration. Presents of money were given to the prisoners we released, to the monasteries and temples, and to the beggars who gathered from miles around. It did much to dispel any lingering animosity.

"After a round of ceremonial farewells we struck tents and marched away. As we started the senior lama and attendants rode up and gave the general a small gilt image of Buddha as a souvenir. He thanked him for his humanity in sparing the temples and monasteries and hoped that whenever he looked at the effigy of Buddha he would always think kindly of Tibet. Then the courteous, cultured priest, a man of generous impulses, shook hands and, mounting his horse, rode slowly away, evidently depressed by the cares of state which now must weigh heavily on his shoulders.

"Three weeks later we emerged from Tibet over the deep snowdrifts of the Nathu-La Pass and descended to the Indian plains. We paused for a last look back up to the towering edge of the icy tableland from which we had come and wondered what we did achieve. Behind us the veil had fallen once again on the forbidden city. Would any white man ever again see the white mice of the Palden Lhamo or watch the lazy line of blue incense rise above the temples of Lhasa? One wondered."

Back in London there was a certain unease about this Younghusband Mission to Tibet, a feeling that it had gone altogether too far, and literally so. A concession reluctantly made, that the mission might cross the frontier, had somehow ended up in the throne room of the Dalai Lama. That was never the intention.

The expedition had been motivated by a fear that the Russians might secretly be establishing a dominating and destabilising influence in Lhasa and thereby upsetting the balance of power in Asia. Now Whitehall was apprehensive that Britain might appear to be exerting political influence in Lhasa and so upsetting the balance herself. What if the Russians now felt constrained to redress that balance?

The most satisfactory course was for Tibet to be removed from the board of Anglo-Russian rivalry altogether.

In 1906 a convention was signed with the Chinese that in effect ascribed responsibility for Tibet to China. Then in 1907 a convention was signed with the Russians whereby both Britain and Russia agreed to recognise the principle of Chinese suzerainty over Tibet. They bound themselves not to send representatives to Lhasa but to deal with Tibet only through the intermediary of the Chinese Government.

Tibet was confirmed as officially out-of-bounds; in effect a buffer between three empires, a no-man's-land. Tibet was not consulted, but then the last time the British had tried to communicate with the Tibetans, it had taken an army, escorting Younghusband, to elicit a response.

And the Russians used 'redressing the balance' as an excuse for annexing Mongolia anyway.

SOURCES

Much of Chapters 2 and 3 is derived from a book called *The Unveiling of Lhasa* by Edmund Candler, a *Daily Mail* correspondent who accompanied the Younghusband Mission and wrote an entertaining and lively account. Also included are paragraphs and phrases from Percival Landon's *Lhasa*. Landon was the *Times* correspondent with the mission. The surgeon accompanying the expedition, Colonel Waddell, wrote *Lhasa and Its Mysteries*, which I have also drawn on. Further material is derived from *Lhasa at Last* by Powell Millington, and from *With the Mounted Infantry in Tibet* by Major W. J. Ottley.

CHAPTER FOUR

The Vanished God-King

The veil of mystery that surrounded Tibet had indeed descended once again. As before adventurers vied to break through that wall of secrecy to Lhasa. But now behind the veil was a British trade agency, at Gyantse. This remote posting provided a unique insight into Tibet. It was also a stepping stone to the senior post of Political Officer, Sikkim, responsible for relations with Tibet.

One February night in 1910 two British sergeants, manning a telegraph post on the Sikkimese border with Tibet, were woken by their servants with the extraordinary news that the Dalai Lama was outside.

Sergeant Luff went to the door. A snowstorm was blowing. In the weak light of a hurricane lamp were seven bedraggled, fur-clad horsemen.

"Which of you blighters is the Dalai Lama?"

The British Army had finally encountered the God-King of Tibet. He was fleeing from the Chinese.

"THERE was no mistaking they were exhausted and very scared. I led them into the hut. He sat down in front of the fire and we gave them all cups of tea. The other fellows all remained standing. They wouldn't sit down in the presence of the boss, even after their long day in the snow. He slept on my bed and two of his fellows slept on the floor in the room in front of the fire."

The next morning, Sergeants Luff and Humphries escorted 'the boss of Tibet', the spiritual overlord of all Central Asia, and his ministers, down the road to the point where the track descends abruptly into the heart of Sikkim on its way to Kalimpong. The whole town turned out to see this mysterious divinity who had appeared out of the blue across the great mountain range. Hindu, Christian and Moslem lined the sides of the road, some bowing, some salaaming. The numerous Buddhists threw their bodies on the ground, prostrating themselves in the dust.

Charles Bell, the British Political Officer in Sikkim, was on his way back from a visit to Bhutan when news of the Dalai Lama's arrival came. He hurried to Darjeeling. Bell spoke fluent Tibetan.

"IT was my duty to look after this most unusual refugee, this incarnation of Buddha, the unknown ruler of Tibet, so I went to see him. The Darjeeling .authorities had accomodated him in a hotel on a central and crowded site, overlooked by the road which ran at the same level as its roof. In one of the largest rooms his attendants had hurriedly contrived a throne. It looked pathetically out of place amongst the European furniture.

"At first sight he did not look like a king; he was small for a Tibetan and dark-skinned, showing his lowly origin, for he was a peasant-farmer's son. (In Tibet things do not happen as elsewhere.) He was, also, completely without the trappings of royalty – no palace, no monks surrounding him, not even the proper clothes, so sudden and rapid was his flight. He was dressed in yellow silks. Mongol boots, made of felt, reached to just below the knee.

"He came down from his seat and put a white scarf of welcome over my wrists, and I one over his. By placing it over my wrists, instead of round my neck, he disclaimed all superiority of rank. He then courteously showed his knowledge of European custom by shaking hands. He had the shaven head of a monk but the alertness of an administrator. His intent brown eyes lit up as he spoke or listened. He looked up at me as if to say, 'What sort of a stranger is this with whom I have to deal from now onwards?'

"Before coming down to business Tibetan custom prescribes a ritual of questions and answers when people go to call on each other. 'Have you not had difficulty on the way?' This seemed ironic after his anxious struggle across the ice-bound uplands in the depths of winter. But custom is inflexible.

"As the Dalai Lama began to tell me why he had fled to India, all those present left the audience chamber.

"In 1904 he had fled to Mongolia, to Urga the capital, a four month journey across the Chang-Tang. From there he continued his wanderings through eastern Tibet and China. In September 1908 he arrived in Peking. (European onlookers had commented on how the huge cavalcade was like a scene from the middle ages; the standard-bearers in the procession, the musicians, the yellow palanquin and especially the band of solemn, red-robed monks.) It was not a happy stay in Peking. The Chinese were censorious and slightening.

"'When I was in Peking,' he said, 'I had received an assurance from the Emperor of China that I would retain my former power and position in Tibet and no harm would be done to the Tibetan people. But the Chinese seemed intent upon converting Tibet into an obedient province of China.'"

"The British mission to Lhasa had been a serious loss of face for the Chinese. They had taken advantage of the disarray and uncertainty that followed the British withdrawal and the absence of the Dalai Lama, to reassert their authority. Confused and dismayed, the Tibetan Government forbade their soldiers to fight. They had no wish for a quarrel with China.

"In December he left Peking and began a slow journey homeward by way of numerous monasteries in the east of Tibet, then back across the cold deserts of the Chang-Tang."

"'Chinese troops were subduing eastern Tibet. They destroyed the great monastery and temple of Batang. Then shortly after I returned to Lhasa, Chinese troops entered the city. I fled. I feared that I would be made a prisoner and deprived of all power. They pursued me and my ministers, offering a reward for our capture.'

"He spoke in a low, quiet voice, with the occasional laugh as when he described how the rearguard, led by the son of an arrowmaker, had held up the Chinese at the Tsang-po ferry.

"'I have come to India to ask the help of the British Government, for unless they intervene the Chinese will occupy Tibet and oppress it, destroy the Buddhist religion and the Tibetan Government and govern the country through Chinese officials. Eventually they will extend their power into the countries that border India and Tibet.'"

"No such visitor had ever descended on India before.

"He was invited to Calcutta to visit Lord Minto, 'The Great Viceroy of the White Expanse', ('White Expanse' meaning India, where people wear white clothes). We went down the little mountain railway. One minister was ill and frightened by the swaying train, until his colleagues laughed it out of him. Viceregal carriages met us at the station to drive us to the great Guest House where Indian princes paying official visits are entertained as guests of the government. The Dalai Lama related his story to the Viceroy and requested British assistance.

"Our visit soon ended and we returned to Darjeeling, the Dalai Lama, a fugitive and impoverished, with apparently no hope of ever returning to his own country.

"The government of India was sufficiently perturbed by these developments on the northern border to protest to Peking. The Chinese retorted that they were simply making effective their suzerainty. The British Government would not intervene between Tibet and China. The order came through from London that our attitude was to be one of strict neutrality.

"The Chinese invasion of Tibet marked a turning point in the relations between the two countries. For centuries the emperors had been careful to do nothing to upset the ancient bond of Priest and Patron. But now, without any hint from the Tibetans of a desire to break with the Empire, an invading force, with modern weapons and contempt for the mystical courtesies of the past, had driven the Dalai Lama from his country and taken over the government. Some Europeans said that he should not have fled but stood by his people in their time of trouble but the Tibetans would point out that by imprisoning him the Chinese would have destroyed the independence of Tibet.

"Within a fortnight of his arrival the excitement caused by such an unusual visitor had subsided and the daily amusements of an Indian hill-station, the polo and tennis, the roller skating and dancing went on as usual.

"The Chinese had meanwhile, for a second time, issued a proclamation deposing the Dalai Lama. The party was full of anxiety as to what the Chinese were doing in Lhasa.

"Tibetans are, however, philosophers. Their religion helps them for it teaches the law of karma, retribution; 'by what ye sow so shall ye reap.' Sooner

Chinese soldiers leaving Gyantse
on deportation to India

or later the oppression of Tibet would recoil on China. They hoped it might be sooner, as indeed it was."

Within a year revolution was breaking out in China – the death throes of the Manchu Empire. In Lhasa, where anyway the invasion had been an administrative failure (no one would co-operate) the Chinese garrison was isolated. Some mutinied, others deserted and tried to make their own way back to China. Others took to looting. Fighting broke out. Eventually the last Chinese were driven out of Tibet by way of India and shipped back to China.

Just two and a half years after his flight to India the Dalai Lama was able to return to Lhasa.

Charles Bell was up early to see the Dalai Lama off on his journey home.

"THE astrologers had fixed an hour well before dawn for the departure of the returning sovereign. These early departures are quite the normal thing in Tibet where, as you lie in bed, you hear the mules pass your bungalow, the bells tinkling as they go.

"My wife and I rode through the deserted Kalimpong marketplace to the residency. Not a soul stirred, not even the pariah dogs. Only the great snow mountains of the Himalaya flickered in the distance, as though eternally on watch.

"It was an hour or more before the pack-mules were ready, but there was no feeling of delay. Among Tibetans time moves freely; it is not harnessed to events. The short figure, closely wrapped up, passed across the verandah in the dark. His shoulders were bowed from spending hours every day, seated cross-legged, reading the sacred books of Buddhism. His ministers were with him. The Dalai Lama and I said our farewells to each other on the verandah, my wife standing at my side. She was careful not to speak to him for that would have offended Tibetan custom. Outside was the golden palanquin, brought down from Lhasa, ready with eight bearers. Thus in the darkness of the night the Precious Sovereign was carried off to take up again the rule of his wide domain.

"Soon after their departure daylight broke. We could see in the distance winding its way up the mountains the gorgeous procession of men, joyful and determined, returning to govern their own land. It was very different from that forlorn arrival of tired men on tired ponies two years before.

The Dalai Lama's palanquin

"In front, astride their ponies, were personal servants with their flat, red, silk hats: behind them the minor officials, priest and lay, in brilliant coloured robes; following them, the members of the Cabinet in their yellow brocades; then the golden chair of state, followed by the three chief ministers, in long crimson cloaks; finally, the lesser lights trailing off into servants at the end.

"'Thus,' the Tibetans said, 'the great sun rose again in the snowy land and the light of happiness spread over the country.'"

"During the exile in Darjeeling the Dalai Lama and I had become close friends. We had spent many hours together in the house that the government had rented for him in a secluded wood. He and his ministers had talked freely of what was happening in Tibet, of their politics, of the mysteries of their complicated religion. Their main fear of the Chinese had been that they would destroy their religion. Its preservation was their one over-riding concern. Even as we talked could be heard, from the room below his, the low

65   The Dalai Lama blessing villagers in the Chumbi Valley

tones of a lama invoking blessings on all living creatures throughout the world. It was my friendship with the Dalai Lama that was eventually to open to me all the secret places of Tibet."

A few months after the Dalai Lama had returned to Tibet, Yuan Shih-Kai, the President of the Chinese Republic, telegraphed him, apologising for the excesses of the Chinese troops and restoring him to his former rank. But the president of a modern republic could never take the place of the Son of Heaven as Patron of the Dalai Lama. The ancient bond of Priest and Patron between Tibet and China had been broken forever. The Dalai Lama replied that he was not asking for any rank. He now intended to exercise both temporal and ecclesiastical rule in Tibet. For Tibet it was the start of 40 years of complete independence.

SOURCES

This chapter is mostly compiled from Charles Bell's *Portrait of the Thirteenth Dalai Lama*. Some paragraphs are from David MacDonald's *Twenty Years in Tibet* and others, especially pages 62, 63 and 66, from Hugh Richardson's *Tibet and Its History*.

CHAPTER FIVE

'The Place of God'

In the years that followed the Dalai Lama's return to Lhasa, Tibetan relations with China continued on the basis of an undeclared and desultory war. The British Government, involved in a world war, kept its distance from Tibetan affairs. Charles Bell was not permitted to accept his open invitation to visit Lhasa. These were difficult times for the Tibetans. Britain appeared indifferent to their pleas for military aid and unable to bring about an agreement with the Chinese over the status of Tibet. The goodwill towards Britain, which Bell's friendship had engendered, waned.

Then in 1919 Bell retired and was preparing to leave for England when the government of India asked him to return to work. They were now somewhat concerned about affairs in Tibet. The Russians were no longer a threat, as they were occupied with their Revolution. But in China militarism was on the rise. A Chinese mission had been in Lhasa and taken every opportunity to lessen British influence. In London it was decided that it was time for a more active encouragement of British relations with Tibet. Bell was instructed to accept the repeated invitations of the Dalai Lama and take a mission to Lhasa.

"I was to convey friendly greetings from the British Government and to explain the state of affairs then prevailing. For more than 20 years I had been working amongst Tibetans; now at last, on the very eve of my retirement, I was to visit the heart of the forbidden kingdom."

"The gales of the Tibetan winter were setting in; it would be cold going over the high passes at that late season but my clerks and servants were excited. They were nearly all Buddhists. 'Our fortune is great that we can visit The Place of the Gods and meet The Lord in His Temple,' they said. By 'The Lord in His Temple', they meant the image of the Buddha in the Jo-Khang.

"From far away on the plains of India, my old friend, Colonel Kennedy, came to join us as doctor to the party. Thus, on November 1, 1920, the day after my 50th birthday, we set out for the Holy City.

"We went to Lhasa by the route through Gyantse and the Tsang-po ferry, the route that Younghusband had taken, 16 years earlier. The cold was intense; there was ice everywhere. After crossing the last pass (over 15,000 feet high) in brilliant winter sunshine, we waited so that we could enter Lhasa on a particularly auspicious day in the Tibetan calendar (in this instance, November 17). This was an absolute necessity, as the Dalai Lama and the Tibetan Government wished to discuss with me matters that they considered vitally important."

"Our entry into Lhasa resembles a triumphant procession. All and sundry have come out several miles to meet us; representatives from Nepal, Bhutan and far Kashmir and members of the powerful nobility. There is a kindly sun but a frostbitten, almost gale-force wind. The endless, unresting dust of Tibet rises thicker and thicker and goes scurrying down the track. Two miles outside the city we are welcomed by the delegates of the Dalai Lama, of the Prime Minister and of the Cabinet. We are conducted to a large tent, with blue designs on the roof after the manner of Tibetan tents, and regaled with tea, biscuits and rice. We stop for ten minutes and pass on, the delegates joining the cavalcade. Further on 100 Tibetan infantry are drawn up and now a party of Ladakhis stand to greet us. Their ancestral homes are three months' journey across the wind-swept, icy plains and passes of western Tibet.

"The crowd grows more and more; the greater part of Lhasa seems to have turned out to see these strange white men who are coming to live amongst them."

Crossing the Tibetan plateau

The Dalai Lama's secretary and his servants

"Lhasa at last! I was the first white man who had ever come to Lhasa at the invitation of the people. In fact I was to stay there longer than any other white man for nearly 200 years.

"Before reaching the Potala we turned right and were conducted to a little house belonging to a former Regent of Tibet, the Head Lama of the monastery of Kundeling, one of the smaller monasteries in Lhasa itself. It was the sort of house where the owners would stay off and on for a few days during the summer to enjoy the fresh air and maybe entertain their friends to archery parties. It lies by the river in its own extensive grounds. The Dekyi-Lingka, 'The Garden of Happiness', was to be home for my year in Lhasa. There was a small garden full of flowers, wild ducks on the river, all tame and friendly, for the Tibetans never kill them, and a large number of willows that kept out the insanitary dust of the city.

"The day after my arrival, the Dalai Lama's secretary, wearing his robes of state and accompanied by his servants, escorted me and my own small retinue to the Norbu-Lingka, 'The Jewel Park', the Dalai Lama's summer palace, to my first interview with the God-King in his own capital. As we passed down the new, well-made road crowds of Tibetans lined the sides. At the entrance to the Norbu-Lingka a military guard in workmanlike khaki uniforms stood to attention. The park was about half a mile square, well-planted with trees and surrounded by a wall. I was received in the Dalai Lama's private apartment. My reception was delightful. He grasped both my hands in his own, and held them for a time, smiling happily at me. 'How glad I am that you have come to Lhasa at last, but what a pity you could not come in the summer, when the flowers are out! Now there are no flowers and the trees are bare.'

"He was simply dressed; a robe of red silk with a yellow jacket underneath, and high, white boots. The room was cold, as are the rooms in Tibetan houses, for here we were in winter at 12,000 feet, without a fire or other heating. But the Dalai Lama's room had one supreme luxury; there was glass in the windows to keep out the Arctic Tibetan wind.

"He had not aged much since I saw him last, eight years ago, except that his eyes had become watery, a condition which his subjects regard as a sign of Buddhahood. He was now 44.

"The Dalai Lama and I sat alone together as we talked. How different was my meeting from that of the Chinese seven months earlier! In their four month stay they had only two meetings, were kept waiting for two hours while they were unceremoniously searched and then they conversed through an interpreter. The Chief Butler brought in tea for us both. My servants then brought in the presents and I handed his Holiness a letter from the Viceroy. Later I would bring the letter from the government of India. This, the first of many interviews, was more ceremonial. It would not be right to discuss political matters yet.

The Norbu-Lingka summer palace   70

The pavilion where the Dalai Lama often sits and works

The Dalai Lama's seat in his private room

Inside the Norbu-Lingka

"After leaving the Dalai Lama I called on my old friend the Prime Minister, Lonchen Sho-kang, who worked in another house in the Norbu-Lingka. An old man now, he spent much of his time in prayer. The Prime Minister, a lay official, is second in rank to the Dalai Lama. He paid his return call on me an hour later. On my enquiring he assured me that were my wife to join me in Lhasa she would be most welcome. However, before the weather was warm enough, events were to render Lhasa dangerous for her to visit.

"Our first month was largely occupied in paying and receiving visits. During this time, we were often in the streets of Lhasa, for in the winter the Tibetan gentry prefer to live in Lhasa rather than in their villas scattered over the neighbouring countryside. Crowds would gather to stare at us as we rode past, but we never met with rudeness.

"The Dalai Lama's chief favourite was Tsarong, whose power outweighed even the Prime Minister's. I had met him during the Dalai Lama's exile in India. Chensa Nang-Kang, as he was then called, was the young man who had held up the pursuing Chinese soldiers during the Dalai Lama's flight. He had then returned to Lhasa and led the Tibetan troops fighting the Chinese in the city. He was a man of lowly birth but of a definite and inflexible purpose. After the Dalai Lama's return to Lhasa the head of the Tsarong family, one of the wealthy noble families of Lhasa, had been put to death for colluding with the Chinese. Chensa Nang-Kang had married Tsarong's daughter and so gained the Tsarong name and estates. Within a very few years he was a member of the Cabinet, Commander-in-Chief of the army and Master of the Mint, the highest in the land.

A Lhasa shopkeeper and her child

A street in Lhasa

"During my year in Lhasa Tsarong and I had many talks together; he was always a good friend to me. He was a great patriot and believed fervently in the superiority of his own people. His manner was somewhat ponderous as compared with the quiet and dignified courtesy of the blue-blooded Tibetan nobles. If his wife was present she teased him gently or otherwise restrained him."

"Life in Lhasa is dominated by the noble families. With the priests they share the higher posts in the administration and, like the monasteries, they own large estates. In theory all land in Tibet belongs to the state which leases it to the nobles. In return they are required to pay revenues to the state, largely in produce but also by service, it being their duty to act as officials of the government. The monasteries, which hold even bigger estates, make their return to the state by prayers and rites for its welfare.

"The nobles owe their origin to one of three sources. The smallest and oldest section of the aristocracy are those who can trace their ancestry right back to the early kings who ruled Tibet several centuries before the Norman conquest of England. Other families (the second group) were perhaps ennobled for some good work done for the country. The third section of the Lhasa nobles are descended from the brothers of previous Dalai Lamas, for the family in which a Dalai Lama takes rebirth is *ipso facto* ennobled and receives a large estate from the government.

A noble family of Lhasa
tracing its descent
for 1400 years

'With the Tibetan Cabinet . . .'
(To Charles Bell's right is
Tsarong Shap-pe and on his
extreme left is Colonel Kennedy.)

In the Finance Office, Lhasa

The Tibetan Cabinet, one monk (left)
and three laymen, in the council chamber

"The nobles are a class apart. There is in many respects a great gulf between them and ordinary folk, who bow down to them and use a different vocabulary in addressing them. But with it all there is a mutual fellowship. Master and mistress, man and maid, all join in the song during an entertainment. In Lhasa one would often meet a party returning from a picnic, husband and wife and servants all walking together."

"Tibet is governed by two separate but parallel administrations, one religious and the other civil. The former consists of 175 specially trained monk officials, the latter 175 hereditary nobles. Many posts are held jointly by a monk and a lay official. The duplication means that each can act as a check on the other and the Church can keep an eye on secular affairs. The two sides of the government converge in the person of the Dalai Lama, the supreme spiritual and temporal ruler.

"The Prime Minister acts as a link between the Kashag (the Cabinet) and the Dalai Lama. The Cabinet consists of three nobles and one monk official, the Kalon Lama, who is the senior member. Almost all government business comes to these Shap-pes, as they are called. The Cabinet office is in the Jo-Khang complex in the centre of Lhasa. The Prime Minister, who does not sit with the Cabinet, passes on its findings to the Dalai Lama, with a note of his own opinion.

"Below the Cabinet are a whole range of government departments; the treasury, the military office, the department supervising the district administration, of which there are about a hundred in Tibet. Though Tibet is a wild and desolate country it is on the whole governed in an orderly manner and the people are well treated under a sort of patriarchal sway.

"To understand the position of the Dalai Lama and the government one must realise that one of the root ideas on which Tibet is based is that it must not be too powerful in a worldly sense. Rich and powerful countries cannot avoid sinning. By killing the inhabitants of the countries they war against they commit great sin. The Tibetans believe that a powerful nation cannot be truly religious.

"Tibet is, as the Dalai Lama put it, 'The Field of Religion'. I could hardly talk to a Tibetan for 15 minutes without the conversation coming round in some way or other to their all-embracing religion.

"I used frequently to visit the Jo-Khang, the great temple, sometimes on the spur of the moment when I happened to be passing by. I had given a golden butterlamp to the temple as one of the presents from the government of India. The lamp was always burning in the Holy of Holies in front of the great image of Buddha brought from China 1,000 years ago.

"I have seen as many as 12,000 monks at a service in the temple, filling the courtyards and surrounding buildings. In Tibet, it is the monks, not the laity, who form the congregation. A few of the laity, pilgrims perhaps, wander in and out to see how the service is going, but take no part in it. The people believe implicitly in the priests and call them in for spiritual help and for medical help too, for illnesses are as a rule ascribed to the action of evil spirits.

"Tibetans regard prayers, reading the sacred books, making certain religious offerings, going round a holy walk in the neigbourhood, and such deeds as amongst the most important parts of religion. His religion puts a background of confidence into the Tibetan's life. The hope to which he aspires is a better rebirth in his next life, and best of all, as a priest in a Buddhist land so he may follow the path more devotedly.

"To the Christian, Love is the highest virtue; to the Buddhist, Wisdom, for they hold that ignorance is the root of all evil. Love, all the same, ranks high; there is no poorhouse or unemployment insurance in Tibet but no poor person will starve, for others will help him as a matter of course.

"That old and experienced administrator, the Prime Minister, summed up religion: 'Do good, not harm, to others – this, just this, is Buddha's teaching. Our Buddhist religion is found in that saying, much more than in monasteries or temples.' Tolerance and loving kindness, both based on Buddhist wisdom, are perhaps the chief reason why the middle way of Gotama Buddha has come down through 2,500 years.

"Tibetan Buddhism is wide in its scope, including all living creatures, however small. A man in this life may have been an ant in the last, and if he does ill, a goose in the next.

"All Tibetans are very fond of birds and the Dalai Lama certainly was. Whenever I visited him there was always a bird or two, perhaps a talking mynah-bird from India, nearby. It is believed that every year the birds hold their parliament at a large lake north of Lhasa, where justice is administered by their king, the cuckoo. Every year the Dalai Lama sends a deputation to this parliament of birds. A lama addresses them on the importance of law and order.

"And like all Tibetans the Dalai Lama was very fond of flowers too. He would spend a large part of his leisure time in his gardens in the Norbu-Lingka, where he sowed and planted with his own hands. I procured packets of seeds for him from Calcutta and London."

"Under the trees in the Norbu-Lingka are a number of animals – monkeys, a musk deer, porcupines, a Bengal tiger. Numerous animals are given to his Holiness. When too many, the excess is handed over to this or that nobleman. They usually do not want them but have to provide a home for them with as good grace as possible. When visiting a leading noble family, I see a box on the verandah and in the box a pair of guinea pigs.

"'Where did these come from?' I ask.

"With a wry but good-humoured smile comes the reply, 'They belong to the Inmost One. He does not want them and has told us to look after them.'

"The bystanders laugh merrily."

"Now that I had come to their capital the Tibetans were hoping that we would give them some substantial help against Chinese aggression towards Tibet. They had suffered from both invasion and domination in the past. 'China,' they said, 'can show no treaty or other document proving that Tibet is under China.'

"There were about 6,000 men in the so-called regular army, scattered throughout Tibet. They were hardy but had no real military training; their rifles and ammunition were poor, being manufactured in a primitive work-

Blacksmiths working in the Lhasa arsenal

shop outside Lhasa. Besides, Buddhism, with its prohibition on taking life, makes the work of a soldier difficult. I pointed out that they therefore had very little chance of protecting the country from Chinese invasion and it seemed to me that the number should be increased to about 15,000.

"The Dalai Lama put the proposal to the National Assembly. The National Assembly is the nearest thing in Tibet to a parliament, an example of the semi-democratic nature of the Tibetan Government. It includes all 350 lay and secular officials who happen to be stationed in or near Lhasa. When summoned by the Prime Minister, on the orders of the Dalai Lama, they assemble in a large, bare, dark room with plank flooring on an upper storey of the Jo-Khang, near the Cabinet Office. On a raised portion sit the higher officials. The members sit on rugs on the floor. High up on the walls are openings of wooden lattice-work to let in light and air, but the proceedings cannot be heard outside, nor would anybody be allowed to go to the walls and listen.

"The abbots and treasurers of the three great monasteries of Lhasa, Drepung, Ganden and Sera, attend and exercise great influence, for they speak for 20,000 monks who are close at hand and may often be turbulent. Some among those who do manual work for the government, mostly carpenters and tailors, are given civil rank and are entitled to attend. The

priests usually speak more than the laymen, who hold large estates that go with their post and cannot afford to offend the government. The celibate priests who have neither family nor property to consider can say pretty well what they wish. There are no regular speeches, rather a general conversation. There is no vote. From the way the discussion continues the prevalent opinion becomes apparent and then this is communicated to the Cabinet and thence to the Dalai Lama by the Prime Minister. During the two and a half centuries which preceded the present Dalai Lama's coming of age, the Parliament exercised great power in Tibet. Nowadays, the Dalai Lama, concerned to introduce reforms, was becoming increasingly autocratic and would often disagree with Parliament's recommendation and give another order. 'The Parliament goes on talking and talking,' the Dalai Lama would tell me, 'and makes great delay in cutting the cord [deciding].'"

"The proposal to increase the army is strongly disliked by the monks who feel that it is against the Buddhist religion. They also suspect, naturally enough, that the army will in time lessen their own power.

"The Assembly proposes that 5 or 600 soldiers should be recruited each year, raising the numbers gradually, and that the monastic estates and the estates of the nobility should be taxed to provide the pay for the soldiers. These proposals cause alarm amongst the people who fear not only that taxes will be increased but that monks will be recruited and the religion thus dishonoured. The nobility, too, looks on military service as a degradation and despair lest their sons be recruited as officers. However, the Dalai Lama is determined to put the plan through, despite the opposition."

The Lord Chamberlain

"Meanwhile the Dalai Lama was busy with a great many other matters. 'The Great Prayer', the largest and most important of the religious festivals, was approaching. The Precious Sovereign must leave the seclusion of the Norbu-Lingka to live for a time in the historic Potala. Only occasionally did he now stay in the Potala as had former Dalai Lamas. 'I find no privacy while living there,' he later told me, 'and no exercise but walking on the roof. There are many steps to climb as it is built into the hill. They merely take one down into the dust and smell of the city.'

"It was not the Dalai Lama's habit to overstate the case nor did he do so on this occasion. There are ten or 12 religious festivals every year in Lhasa. In the larger ones the population of 15 to 20,000 may be swollen, with monks and pilgrims, to five times that number and so it remains for two or three weeks. There are no sanitary arrangements of any kind: in the houses a hole in the floor; outside, just dark corners in the streets and the surrounding fields. The raging winds of Tibet carry the dust of this dry climate and the germs with it."

"The journey to the Potala is made in state. The Dalai Lama believes in pageantry; it is good for the religion, for the country, for himself. He is very pleased when told that it also appeals to us British.

"The entire population of Lhasa lines the route of the procession. The bodyguard and the Lhasa soldiers line the foot of the Potala hill. There are the ladies of the leading families of Lhasa, in their gorgeous silk robes, aprons of many-coloured stripes and headdresses sewn with corals, turquoise and seed pearls. Parties of townsmen and villagers crowd the mile-long route, monks hold up sacred banners. All is now ready for the solemn procession. Then a caravan of little Tibetan donkeys, carrying their wares to Lhasa, plods patiently along the road. Nobody resents their appearance at this supreme moment or thinks that they may interfere with the cavalcade that is to follow. Smoke rises from incense burners in the distance, meaning that the Dalai Lama has started."

"The Great Prayer lasts for three weeks, following the commencement of the New Year. It is a prayer for the good of all human beings and the whole of the animal kingdom throughout the world, but especially it is a blessing for the happiness of the people of Tibet. For the duration of the prayer, the 20,000 monks of the surrounding monasteries descend into Lhasa and formally take over the running of the city.

"Most of the monks are indeed devoted to their religion. But there is a large body of monks who are in effect professional fighters and people hire them as bodyguards. They are likely to break into fighting during the crowded

festivals. In the months leading up to the Great Prayer there is indeed great friction between the monasteries and the soldiery in Lhasa.

"All are afraid of a clash between the two, and many are hiding away their property in the villages around Lhasa. There are rumours that the British Government is sending troops to the Holy City to aid the Tibetan soldiers against the monks. The great monasteries are on the point of breaking into rebellion. Feelings are acutely inflamed. The atmosphere is electric. Tsarong is in a highly excited condition. As head of the army, he is highly unpopular and hated by the monks. He fears that he will be assassinated. He carries a loaded revolver wherever he goes.

"Many of the monks are asking who it is who has brought the British to Lhasa. Placards are put up in various places telling the people to kill Kennedy and myself. The placards are pulled down before we see them. The Dalai

Lama is nervous as trouble in Lhasa would give the Chinese a pretext for sending troops, saying they must restore law and order – this in spite of the Tibetan Government on the whole governing Tibet in a much more orderly manner than the Chinese Government China. But though an outbreak threatens it is unthinkable that any of the religious observances of the prayer festival should be abandoned.

"I suggest to the Dalai Lama that now that he has 6,000 soldiers it must surely be easier to keep the large monasteries in order. 'But easier still,' he replies, 'by my carefully choosing their heads and the heads of the colleges into which they are divided.'"

"The Great Prayer passed off, however, without untoward event and his Holiness returned to the Norbu-Lingka; but the tension had not lessened. The Dalai Lama thought the situation so grave that he ordered his Chief Secretary to make an investigation. He received the report and came to a decision, but this was kept secret until it was made known at 'The Presence Tea'. The Presence Tea is a gathering held each afternoon at the Norbu-Lingka and lasting about half an hour. All officials in Lhasa from the Grand Secretaries downwards must attend. The Dalai Lama seldom does so, his officials taking charge. Tea is drunk, for the giving of tea is an auspicious omen, just as in a household the servants should be entertained periodically by their master to increase its happiness and prosperity. But no talking is permitted, except in low tones. It is in effect a kind of roll call, to ensure that the priest officials at Lhasa do not go away on their own pleasure or business.

"On March 26, The Presence Tea was evidently of unusual importance, for the Cabinet Ministers were ordered to attend it. The reason soon became known. The Chief Secretary read out the Dalai Lama's orders. One of the Cabinet Ministers, Kun-sang-tse, was dismissed. He had been found guilty of being at the bottom of the trouble and of hiding his property. Two other members of the Cabinet were fined. Three colonels were dismissed for taking part in a quarrel with the Financial Commissioners. Two junior military officers, one of them the Dalai Lama's nephew, were fined for lesser offences. Others were punished to a smaller degree. The Cabinet Minister had to take off his uniform – hat, robe and boots – immediately. One of his colleagues managed to find the dress of a lesser member of the nobility for him to go home in, for evidently he had had no idea of what was in store for him. On his way to the Norbu-Lingka he had passed Kennedy and cheerfully waved to him.

"The Chief Secretary, on the Dalai Lama's behalf, also warned the monk magistrates to keep the monks under strict control during the second religious

festival of the year which was to take place shortly. He impressed upon them the injury that would result to the monasteries if fighting broke out and left them in no doubt that the Dalai Lama would punish them severely. The whole of Lhasa was talking over the matter. This otherwise painful affair had one humorous aspect that caused much merriment. The Dalai Lama ordered that all valuables removed from Lhasa were to be left where they were.

"'The Precious Protector's power is very great nowadays,' said a friend of mine, pleased and somewhat surprised that the Dalai Lama should be able go as far as he does.

"Popular opinion in Tibet is deeply concerned with the strict observance of custom. There are no newspapers in Tibet. Criticism is voiced in a typically Tibetan way; women labourers loudly and merrily sing often witty, allusive and pointed lampoons on the acts of their rulers. By tradition they enjoy complete immunity. They sing even in the presence of the object of their attack. In this way, what the people are thinking soon becomes known all over the city.

"Some time afterwards I was riding along the broad road from the Norbu-Lingka to the Potala. It was crowded with priest officials and their servants returning from their daily Presence Tea, and with labourers returning from their day's work. A party of women labourers were protesting in song. No one restrained them from doing so as it would be against the custom. In their song they asked why the colonels and other army officers had been punished and Tsarong not. Tsarong had tried to resign his government posts but the Dalai Lama had refused.

"The feeling against me seemed to be gradually cooling down. The Dalai Lama honoured me and I was gaining the good will of the people by studying and observing Tibetan customs, as well as Tibetan etiquette, which to them is so important. And the increase of the army was being put through in, as the Dalai Lama said, 'a gentle manner.'"

"Eventually the time comes when I tell the Dalai Lama that I shall soon be leaving for India where I expect to see the Viceroy and the Foreign Secretary, and that shortly after that I shall go back to England on retiring from government service.

"All the Tibetans are delighted that the British Government has accepted all my recommendations for the betterment of our relations with Tibet. These include the extension of the telegraph line from Gyantse to Lhasa, thus putting the Holy City in telegraphic communication with the outside world. The Tibetans are also to be permitted to import a certain quantity of arms and obtain some help with military training.

"Because we are leaving soon, we give a few small presents to our Tibetan friends. Amongst other things we make a distribution of flower seeds to various people and to monasteries, because they are all so fond of flowers. But we cannot give flowers to the three great monasteries, for they are not allowed to grow them. Such pleasures are regarded as likely to entice them from their exceptionally important religious duties. They are not even allowed to read books on history, lest they find them too interesting and thereby be enticed from the reading of their Buddhist scriptures. Narrow is the gate, and narrow the road that is marked out for their spiritual life, though, like the followers of Christ, many stray from it."

"I am to take the Dalai Lama's photograph, in the throne room in the Norbu-Lingka. It is the first time that anyone has photographed him in the Holy City.

"The throne is four feet high, a seat without back or arms. On the wall behind and above are nine silk scrolls representing Buddha. Hanging down in front of the throne is a cloth of rich white silk, handsomely embroidered in gold, with the crossed thunderbolts of the God of Rain. Chrysanthemums, marigolds and other flowers are arranged round the dais. This is the throne used on important occasions.

"When I arrive at the appointed hour the room is not ready. I watch them arranging it. The Dalai Lama comes in to see that it is correctly done. He is simply and comfortably dressed as is his custom when not engaged in ceremonies or public functions. Monk officials and ordinary workmen go about their work, almost jostling him, while he winds in and out amongst them, giving an order here, making a slight change there. Workmen clean and polish the boarded floor by sliding over it in their Tibetan boots with large woollen pads attached. For anyone who does not know him, it would be hard to say who the Dalai Lama is, so inconspicuously does he move among them. Though a God-King there is a simplicity about his everyday life."

"Tibetans believe in good and bad luck. Everybody has two lucky days and one unlucky day each week. These all depend on which year, out of the cycle of 12 animals, he is born in. The Dalai Lama was born in the Mouse Year so his lucky days are Tuesday and Wednesday, and his unlucky one Saturday. On Saturday, therefore, government work is not carried out in Tibet, the

The Dalai Lama on his throne in the Norbu-Lingka

public offices being closed on that day as, in Christian lands, they are closed on Sundays. I have chosen to leave Lhasa on one of the lucky days of the Dalai Lama, which gives great pleasure to the people and is expected to insure us against illness and accident.

"During my last few days in Lhasa I exchange farewell visits with the ministers and other leading Tibetans who call on me. I pay my farewell visit to the Dalai Lama, a sad parting for both of us. 'I want you to write to me from time to time after you go to England,' he says to me. Tsarong calls at our house to say his farewells, too. He is taking a little to such European customs.

"As we depart, the receptions, guards of honour and so on are similar to those on our arrival, but there is one notable exception. The Dalai Lama himself comes out of his seclusion and stands on the roof of a neighbouring house to see us pass down the road, although he is in full view of the crowd of people that throng the roadside to witness our departure. I wave my farewells to him as I pass, and he bows and smiles in return. Such an action on the part of a Dalai Lama is perhaps unprecedented in the annals of Tibet.

"For three days the senior monk official from the Potala accompanies us, to the foot of the Kam-pa La Pass. Others continue with us to Gyantse where we say our farewells. In accordance with Tibetan etiquette, we say to each other, 'I must petition you that we may meet again from time to time.' This is said though they and I know that it is improbable that we shall ever meet again."

"The Viceroy wrote officially to the Dalai Lama thanking him and the Tibetan Government for their friendly treatment of me. In his reply, over his large, red, square, official seal, the Dalai Lama expressed his great pleasure at the Viceroy's letter and wrote, 'All the people of Tibet and myself have become of one mind, and the British and Tibetans have become one family.'

"It would not be fair to compare the Dalai Lama's rule with that of rulers in western countries. Tibet is still in the feudal stage of development. Certainly the Tibetans would not be happy if they were governed as people are in England; and it is probable that they are on the whole happier than are people in Europe and America under their own governments. Great changes will come in time, but unless they come slowly, when the people are ready to assimilate them, they will cause great unhappiness. Meanwhile, it remains to stress that the general administration of Tibet is more orderly than the administration in China; the Tibetan standard of living is higher than that of China or India; and the status of women in Tibet is higher than their status in either of those two large countries.

"My aim had been that Tibet should enjoy internal autonomy, free to live her own life, and in her freedom be the best possible barrier for the northern frontier of India.

"With my mission over I left for England which had become a half-forgotten country."

SOURCES

This chapter is mostly derived from Charles Bell's *Portrait of the Thirteenth Dalai Lama*. Other material, especially page 85, is from Hugh Richardson's *Tibet and Its History*.

The Prime Minister's daughter with a friend   89

CHAPTER SIX

'For the Welfare of the Inside'

The constant aim of British policy with regard to Tibet was to maintain the peaceful state of affairs beyond the northern frontier. Unlike the North-West Frontier with Afghanistan, the frontier with Tibet was virtually unmanned. There was no threat from hostile forces of any sort on the whole of that long border that stretched from Assam in the east to Ladakh 2,000 miles to the west.

In the interest of India it was important that a settlement to any disputes between Tibet and China should be found. Any hope that Bell's visit to Lhasa, by in effect treating Tibet as an independent country, might prompt the Chinese into negotiations about the status of Tibet came to nothing. The central government in China at the time was weak and the border areas were riven by feuds. But to the Chinese, Tibet's de facto *independence was irrelevant; Tibet was simply part of China.*

Three years after Bell's visit, his successor, Frederick Bailey, paid a short visit to Lhasa. He had spent many years on the Tibetan borderlands since he'd first gone to Lhasa with the Younghusband expedition 20 years earlier.

Bailey had friendly talks with the Dalai Lama, about relations with China and about the Dalai Lama's plans for limited modernisation. He was only the second European ever to be invited to Lhasa.

For many years there had been rivalry between the central authority of Lhasa and the court of the Panchen Lama, Tibet's other great spiritual leader, at the huge monastery of Tashilhunpo near Shigatse, the second largest town of Tibet. A modest and gentle man, the Panchen Lama was much loved throughout Tibet and particularly so in the neighbourhood of his monastery. Lhasa insisted that Tashilhunpo was subordinate but the monastery had become accustomed to considerable administrative independence. A rift was inevitable. In 1923 the Panchen Lama, in despair, fled to China where he was warmly received. The Dalai Lama was more than a little disturbed. The flight caused great disquiet throughout Tibet. It was to be the source of much trouble over the ensuing years.

The Dalai Lama found he could no longer ignore the determined opposition of the monasteries to his modern ideas. They particularly resented the army

and police which, they felt, challenged the rightful supremacy of religion. *Anxious to show that he was not under outside influence, the Dalai Lama turned away from ideas associated with Britain. The police and army fell into decay. Tsarong lost most of his power and was degraded. An English school at Gyantse was closed. Not for another seven years was a Political Officer invited to Lhasa.*

It was trouble with Nepal that eventually prompted the Dalai Lama to try to re-establish friendly relations with the British. He invited Leslie Weir, Bailey's successor, to visit Lhasa in 1930 and again in 1933 when there was serious trouble on the far-distant and contentious border with China. What had started as a dispute between two monasteries led to a Chinese warlord siding with one and the Tibetans siding with the other. The fighting got out of hand and the Dalai Lama appealed to the British for help. But by the time Weir arrived in Lhasa the Chinese on the border had fallen to warring amongst themselves and had readily agreed to a ceasefire with Tibet.

Meanwhile in China the Nationalist government of Chiang Kai-shek was beginning to find its feet and was working out far-reaching plans for restoring its sovereignty over Tibet. It had no thoughts of involving Britain in any agreement it was going to make with Tibet.

Charles Bell, in retirement in England, corresponded regularly with the Dalai Lama. In the autumn of 1933 he and his wife and daughter were in Kalimpong.

"WE were hoping to go to Lhasa, on a private visit, as soon as the passes over the mountain ranges were open. We were having tea with David MacDonald, for so many years the trade agent at Gyantse, in the little hotel that his daughter was running there, when the blow struck. A note was handed to MacDonald; the Dalai Lama had 'retired to The Heavenly Field', that is, had passed out of his 13th incarnation.

"It would be true to say that this selfless ruler, born to a shepherd family, died of overwork in the service of his country. The first Dalai Lama for nearly 100 years actually to rule his people, he had been a good ruler, both secular and spiritual. He had instigated many reforms, improved law and order, and the standard of the priesthood, ensuring that the priests kept to their studies and diminishing their interference in politics. He took care of the innumerable religious buildings and on the whole increased the spirituality of Tibetan Buddhism. In the hope of preventing Chinese domination he built up the army in the face of priestly opposition. During his reign he abolished Chinese domination entirely throughout the large part of Tibet governed by him. His people were grateful for the strength of his government.

"Traders coming down from Tibet with their yearly supply of wool, yak tails, skins and other products, brought stories of the Precious Protector's death. He had died on a Sunday. According to Tibetan notions this is an evil omen. They said too that he died on a stormy night, and that portends sickness and calamity for Tibet. The people were dismayed and disorientated by his departure.

"Before he passed to The Heavenly Field the Dalai Lama wrote, in his own hand, a letter to his people. It was printed on the usual Tibetan hand-carved wooden blocks; a book of nine small pages.

"'. . . Do not be traitors to Church and State by working for others against your own,' he instructed his people. 'Tibet is happy and in comfort now; the matter rests in your hands. All must act in harmony to bring happiness to Tibet. You have heard what the red people have done in Mongolia where religion is destroyed. Unless we can guard our own country, the monasteries and the priesthood, their lands and properties, will be destroyed and all will be sunk in great hardship and in overpowering fear; the days and nights will drag slowly in suffering. For the welfare of the inside (Tibet) keep the law and custom and do your work in the spirit of the Lord Buddha. Then Tibet will remain happy and prosperous . . .'"

The interim government, hesitant and anxious, consciously set themselves to change nothing. A Chinese mission was allowed to come to Lhasa, on the pretext of offering condolences. Its real object was to see whether, now the Dalai Lama was gone, the Tibetans could be brought under Chinese rule. Negotiations about frontier disputes were eventually started. But on the matter of their independence the Tibetans were obdurate and the Chinese left with their mission unfulfilled. However they left behind in Lhasa two officers with a wireless set. In time this became a de facto diplomatic mission.

The Chinese had a foothold back in Lhasa.

This chapter is mostly derived from Hugh Richardson with material on pages 92–4 from Bell's *Portrait of the Thirteenth Dalai Lama*.

Villagers threshing at Ralung

CHAPTER SEVEN

The 1936 Mission to Lhasa

Some two months after the death of the Dalai Lama the Cabinet appointed as Regent of Tibet the young head lama of Reting, an ancient monastery 60 miles north of Lhasa. In 1935 Weir's successor as Political Officer in Sikkim, Frederick Williamson, and his young wife Margaret, came up from India to greet the Regent on his installation. They joined the crowds on the banks of the Kyi-Chu river down which the Regent came in a coracle and watched the huge procession that escorted him in a palanquin to the Potala, with the bands playing and monks carrying banners, riding on ponies.

The main reason for Williamson's visit to Lhasa was to try to mediate in a dispute between the Tibetans and the Chinese over the return of the Panchen Lama. The dispute concerned the proposal that the lama should return to Tibet with a Chinese military escort. The Tibetans were steadfastly opposed to that. The affair was causing considerable anxiety.

Williamson had been ill for some time and eventually died in Lhasa. To counter any possible lack of prestige brought on by the death of its emissary to Tibet, the government of India decided to send a large mission to Lhasa. It was headed by Sir Basil Gould who took over Williamson's duties as Political Officer in Sikkim.

Freddy Spencer Chapman, a mountaineer and photographer, went along as private secretary to Gould and as official diarist.

"THERE were to be eleven of us in all. Phillip Neame (V.C.) was to give the Tibetans such advice as they might need on military matters. Hugh Richardson, recently appointed trade agent at Gyantse, was to come on with us to Lhasa. We were all to meet at the Residency in Gangtok.

"The train left the sweltering heat of Calcutta at 9.00 pm in the evening of July 27, 1936, and reached Siliguri at 6.30 the following morning. When I woke up at 6 we were still crossing the interminable plain of Bengal. But already, with growing excitement, I could see ahead the misty blue line of the Himalayan foothills. From Siliguri the narrow motor-road winds up and up through the forest. The air grew cool and fresh. Suddenly above the high, forested ridges there was a glimpse of far-off snows. We had reached Gangtok, capital of Sikkim. A mile outside the town was the Residency."

"Three days later our party of 50 horsemen and 200 mules set out on the long trek to Lhasa. There is always a feeling of liberation in setting off with a few chosen companions on a carefully planned expedition, but there was something especially dramatic about beginning this journey to the holy and forbidden city. It was a place almost nobody went to."

"Buddhist prayerflags fluttered beside the track, the golden roof of the Maharaja's palace shining in the sunlight in Gangtok, far below now, and ahead the fir-clad hillsides rose steeply, hill behind hill, into the clouds. Above them was Tibet."

"Three and a half weeks after leaving Gangtok we are camped on a grassy field by the Kyi-Chu river, near the tomb of Atisha at Nethang, a day's journey from Lhasa. There are hoopoes and ibis-bills and ringed plovers by the water. Two coracles swish by, one laden with earthenware pots, another with skins of butter. There was a lot of traffic on the road today, mostly yaks laden with wool. Many of the men carry antiquated flintlock guns with projecting prongs of antelope horn to use as a rest when firing. Others carry swords in silver scabbards set with turquoise and coral. They are grand-looking men, swarthy and independent as Bedouins. They are very cruel to their animals. There were many monks on the road, too. They often carry their boots to save wear.

"Earlier today we were met by a monk official who is to be one of our guides. He is a very polished and intelligent man. Oddly enough his mulberry-coloured monk's robe, which is quite new, has small patches on it, not because it is torn but I suppose to indicate conventional poverty. He rides a fine pacing mule and wears a remarkable wide-brimmed hat of papier-mâché, covered in gold lacquer."

'Swarthy and independent
as bedouin . . .'

The lama guide from Lhasa meeting the
Mission near Jangme.

Mission Camp at Netang our march
from Lhasa.

A page from
Philip Neame's
photograph album

Two officials
in ceremonial
new year costume ▶

"August 24. The road to Lhasa climbs steeply between flat-roofed houses past granite spurs gay with prayerflags and wall-paintings. Most of the villagers have come out to have a look at us. They are incredibly dirty and ill-clad; many have goitres. The children are stark naked. Everybody seems very cheerful and friendly.

"Just short of the Drepung monastery we are welcomed on behalf of the Tibetan Government by Mondo, a monk official, who, by the most remarkable anomaly, is an Old Rugbeian. In 1913, at the request of the Dalai Lama, Gould, who was then acting trade agent at Gyantse, took four boys to be educated in England. After Rugby they trained respectively as soldier, surveyor, mining and electrical engineer. Mondo, the mining engineer, having tried unsuccessfully to overcome the prejudice of the monks to his activities, has returned to more normal work. He is a large, genial man with cropped hair and a moustache. He still speaks the most delightful English, perfectly pronounced. We are also met and presented with scarves by our lay guide, a young official wearing a flowered-silk robe the colour of fallen beech leaves; over it, a scarlet gown lined with pale blue. His flat-topped hat of yellow wool balances on top of his head like a porridge bowl.

"We are soon met by more officials, all most courteous and friendly, and full of solicitous enquiries about our health and the discomfort of the journey. Half the population of Lhasa has come down to see us arrive.

"A company of soldiers and another of police, complete with flying colours and two military bands, are drawn up as a guard of honour. They present arms and so on while Gould is presented to the officers. They look incongruous in khaki uniforms and battered topees, with huge earrings and long pigtails. But they march and drill better than one would have expected.

"Had anyone told me a year ago that I should be in Lhasa today, I would not for a moment have believed them."

"As had the preceding missions we stayed in the Dekyi-Lingka. Our first four days were taken up with a continuous stream of callers, a kaleidoscopic procession of gorgeously clad monk and lay officials, from the Prime Minister to the lowest government secretary.

"First to arrive was Yuto Depon, a young army general, who delivered scarves of greeting and presents from the Cabinet Ministers. He was dressed in the smartest of British-made military uniforms, but wore a long turquoise earring and had his hair tied with a red ribbon into a double topknot with a turquoise and gold charmbox in the centre. It is an ornament worn by all government officials. Neame congratulated him on the turnout of the guard of honour but Yuto disclaimed all credit, saying that he was afraid that the Brigadier might laugh at the drill and uniform of the soldiers.

"Next came the three lay members of the Cabinet. They were preceded by their secretaries and servants, on horseback, who came splashing through the floodwater of our drive. The Shap-pes rode in slowly in order of seniority.

The mission on its last march into Lhasa

They were splendidly dressed in saffron-yellow silk robes, interwoven with dragon patterns. They sat cross-legged on divans in our reception room. Langchungna, the most senior through having served the longest, rarely said anything, except to agree with the others. He had an expression of good-natured complacency. When he smiled his eyes disappeared. Very conservative, he kept saying that Lhasa is not what it was when he was a boy, especially with regard to the weather, the deterioration of which, he declared, coincided with the installation of electricity in the city. Nobody quite knows why the Dalai Lama made him a Shap-pe; he is neither of noble family nor of conspicuous brilliance.

Langchungna Shap-pe   Bhondong Shap-pe

Tendong Shap-pe   The Lord Chamberlain   104   Dzaza Gundeling and the Kalon Lama

"Much younger was Bhondong Shap-pe. He had a fat face and a ready grin. As he was for many years secretary to the Cabinet and won his way to his present position, he had a great knowledge of the Lhasa methods of government. He is a genuine fellow and undoubtedly efficient.

"Tendong Shap-pe was a governor in Kham for many years and has the reputation of being a great fighter. He is a large-featured and rather ugly man, of great natural charm and distinction. His skin is deeply pitted with smallpox scars. The disease is the scourge of Tibet.

"To me the meeting had an air of unreality, tea and cake being served – Gould, immaculate in Saville Row suit, smilingly making conversation, on one side, with Norbu, our interpreter, swallowing his words with excitement; on the other, the three Shap-pes of Tibet bowing in unison and smiling deferentially at each remark.

"In the afternoon came the fourth, and by virtue of being a monk, the senior member of the Cabinet, the Kalon Lama. He wore his terra-cotta monk's robe over the top of his yellow Shap-pe's silk. He seemed a mild and courteous old man of no special distinction. He said that the political situation was indeed serious, but that he didn't know what to do about it. After all, he said, he was a peaceful monk and what was he to know about Chinese escorts and machine guns? Actually, I guessed he knew more than one would have thought.

"Among our many visitors was the owner of our house, the head of the neigbouring Gundeling monastery, Dzaza Gundeling. 'Dzaza' is a title

conferred on monks and laymen who have rendered particularly meritorious service to the state. He is a most impressive man, very tall for a Tibetan and vigorous in spite of his advanced age. He has a deeply-lined face, full of character and determination. Though he has a charming, gentle manner, he is obviously one of the most forceful personalities in Lhasa, a leading power in the National Assembly.

"We also received a visit from the Lord Chamberlain, a very aged lama who is supreme head of the ecclesiastical organisation of Tibet. He is also the chief official of the Dalai Lama's household, responsible for the upkeep of the Potala and in charge of the Lhasa parks.

"He is a frail and courteous old man who suffers from rheumatism and overwork. Soon after him came the grand secretaries for clerical affairs, four monk officials who compose what is virtually the Lama Cabinet. One of these is Commander-in-Chief of the Tibetan Army, which seems a curious position for a monk to hold.

"Another interesting visitor was the Oracle who, when in a trance, is consulted by the government on important matters of state. He lives in the Nechung Temple near the Drepung monastery. Despite his profession, he seemed very much a man of the world and invited us to come and visit his temple.

"The most interesting visitor of all was Tsarong Dzaza, who came on a friendly call, with his wife. He holds no official position now but is the leading figure in the National Assembly and, at a time when a general air of indecision and uncertainty prevails, assumes the position of the strong man of Lhasa.

The mission before calling
on the Regent

The Regent blessing
the mission servants

The Regent listening to the gramophone

"He is a thickset, jovial man, getting rather short of teeth and hair. The Tsarongs called formally on the Political Officer and then, as another visitor arrived, went to present their compliments to Richardson. We all of us forgathered there and spent a happy hour laughing and joking and discussing every sort of subject, as if we had known each other for years. Tsarong's wife is perfectly self-assured and charming and, as we found later, a perfect hostess. We gathered from Tsarong that the Tibetans were extremely worried."

"Two days after our arrival at Lhasa we rode in solemn procession to pay a call on the Regent and the Prime Minister at the Potala. Leaving our ponies at the gateway we threaded our way along dark passages to an anteroom where officials took charge of us. The Regent's throne room was small, with frescoes on the wall and a row of religious banners hanging above the throne. We presented scarves and then sat on low cushions while tea, biscuits and dried fruit were handed round by two colossal monks. First our clerks were presented to the Regent who blessed each in turn. Then Gould and the Regent had a formal conversation. It was an impressive interview though the Regent had little presence. He is a frail, undersized monk of 23. When we went he got up and shook hands with each of us in turn. He was most unaffected and simple and rather wearied by the greatness thrust upon him. He complained that he could get no exercise because he was carried everywhere in a palanquin. Later we discovered that he has started playing football with one of the huge monk bodyguards. He sent round to ask whether we had a spare ball. This alone seemed to justify our mission.

"We could never quite fathom the extent of the Regent's influence, or in what direction it was exerted. He always seemed to be very friendly to us and declared his intention to visit India some day but rumour had it that he was in communication with China."

"For several days we were kept busy returning calls and delivering presents. In every case we were most hospitably entertained and continually delighted by the dignified courtesy and urbanity of each official we met. Each house gives evidence of the highly developed artistic skills of the Tibetans in architecture and interior decoration. There are exquisite examples of their carving and painting and metalwork in every room, particularly in the private chapel which is usually the best room in the house and often the room where we were entertained.

"The Tsarong's magnificent mansion lies near the river, on the road between the Potala and the Prime Minister's house. Between these, the dwellings of the two highest people in the land, we had to splash through stinking puddles and past heaps of the foullest imaginable carrion and garbage. It can only be the cold, dry climate that prevents an outbreak of disease.

"In most Tibetan houses we had to be on our best behaviour but Tsarong's parties are always completely riotous, especially when his three children come home from school. Tibetan children are most delightful, quite unspoilt, and full of life and intelligence. During our visit we had a children's party. We were much struck by how charmingly they behaved to each other. If a child was unable to master the difficulties of spoon and fork his neighbour helped him. When one child spilt his curry in his lap the others laughed with him, not

Mrs. Tsarong with the children

(*left*) Tsarong with his family

Four noble ladies, one
with a Gyantse headdress

at him, and helped him to clear it up. They laugh without reserve but avoid becoming boisterous. A Tibetan mother never says, 'don't,' but the child doesn't anyway. A four-year-old girl fearlessly holds a firework while her six-year-old brother, who has been told to behave exactly like his father, smokes a cigarette with obvious enjoyment.

"The children's schooling is somewhat primitive. They are taught to read and write and recite passages from the Buddhist scriptures, and the elements of arithmetic, but they know nothing of geography or of history, except in so far as it relates to their religion.

"In Lhasa there are only two government schools. Both are for budding officials. The college in the Potala is really a civil service college and trains young monk officials. There is a similar one in the centre of the town, for lay officials. They are taught how to keep accounts and write letters. But besides this there are many private schools and the noble families keep a private tutor who is usually a monk. So excellent a mixture of feudalism and democracy is Tibet that the sons of tenants and servants also attend the classes. At the school kept by the monk telegraphist, I used to see the children, sitting cross-legged on the floor, writing from memory passages from the scriptures. Sometimes they repeated prayers. One day they were all reading aloud, but no two seemed to be reading the same thing. When the telegraphist had to be at his work one of the senior boys looked after the class."

"Neame, alas, could only be spared from his military duties in India long enough to be three weeks in Lhasa. He was very busy finding out about that remarkable organisation, the Tibetan Army. Yuto Depon, who came on the day of our arrival with presents from the Cabinet, and Jigme Taring who was married to Mrs. Tsarong's younger sister, are the moving spirits in the army. They both wore smart khaki tunics, with several gold stars. Tibetan officers can chose their own badges. These, with their long, turquoise earrings and charmboxes, added greatly to their attractive appearance.

"The army is recruited on a feudal basis with each landowner having to supply so many recruits. A review of all available troops, about 500, had been arranged so Neame could see them drilling and carrying out range practice. Yuto and Jigme were afraid that the Brigadier would not be impressed.

"It was a blazing hot morning. We were recieved at the barracks, some two miles outside Lhasa, by the Cabinet. Soon afterwards the Prime Minister arrived, surrounded by servants and retainers. As in other countries, the more important an official the later he arrives. As his horse was led in the Shap pes bowed to the waist. It took some time for the Prime Minister to drink his tea and receive the various military officers, for this was the first time he had ever inspected the army or visited the arsenal.

"It was a great day. On the dry stone plain stood a row of large white ornamented tents for the officials. Practically all the inhabitants of Lhasa had turned out to see the fun, including several thousand monks. They stood or sat in a wide circle, protected by umbrellas from the scorching sun. The more enterprising women had opened small stalls where they were selling apricots, greasy-looking cakes, tea and cigarettes. The crowd, which was fairly orderly, was controlled by junior officials and several gigantic monks.

"Soon a column of troops appeared with a band and with their colours held high above them. I am neither musical nor military-minded but I was greatly impressed by these Tibetan bands. They made a very creditable noise with their bugles and big drums and bagpipes. The drill was ragged. Interestingly, the orders were given in English.

"The next item was rifle practice. But as no Lhasa soldier had fired his rifle for the last six years, the sights seemed out of adjustment. The machine-gun fire was more successful though one gun frequently jammed, and only Jigme could persuade it to work while others frequently ran across its line of fire in their enthusiasm. After this we adjourned for a Tibetan lunch in a small room in the barracks, which was decorated in true military fashion with large Chinese drawings of beautiful women.

"In the afternoon two mountain guns were fired. This was the most popular feature of the day. After the report of the gun there was a moment of breathless excitement and if a direct hit was scored it was greeted with cheers from the crowd who had converged in their eagerness so as to leave only a narrow channel for the line of fire. At the end of the day the Prime Minister presented white scarves all round in appreciation of their efforts.

"The following day Neame spent three hours giving the Shap-pes his advice. They wrote down every word but added they would have to refer every suggestion to the Regent and Prime Minister, moreover they didn't know where the necessary money was coming from.

The Prime Minister
watching the show

'Two mountain guns were fired.'

The Tibetan band

Yuto Depon and Jigme Taring

"The total revenue of the Lhasa Government is small. There is no income tax in Tibet and hardly any customs revenue. The main source of cash is from the leasing out of lands. In ordinary years this is sufficient; the Tibetans have no wish to develop their country along western lines. In Tibet religion comes first.

"We were some seven months in Lhasa. The Tibetans got quite used to the mission. Many officials formed the habit of dropping in to the Dekyi-Lingka for tea or supper; and we were on extraordinarily friendly terms with all classes of Tibetan society. There is nothing here of the rigid caste system of the Hindus, the purdha of Mohammedan women, or any taboos on food or drink.

"Gould, a man of tremendous mental activity and with an unbelievable capacity for hard work, was constantly being consulted for advice on political matters. His object was to do all in his power to effect a reconciliation between the Lhasa Government and the Chinese about the Panchen Lama. Gould had frequent and friendly meetings with the Panchen Lama's trusted adviser, who informed him of British anxiety for a peaceful settlement.

"There were frequent rumours that the Panchen Lama had set out on his return to Tashilhunpo, and that a consignment of hand grenades had been found in his advance baggage, but it became clear by the end of January that

Yerpa Hermitage

Ladies of the Shigatse family
of Dele Rabden

Gymaa thri khang, a district headquarters

his return was as remote as ever. The Tibetans would not agree to a Chinese military escort and we were forced to realise that either he was so much indebted to China that he was no longer a free agent or that the officials of his entourage, wedded to Chinese wives, and in the generous pay of the Chinese Government, were reluctant to hazard an uncertain welcome in Tibet without the Chinese escort.

"Gould decided that there was nothing more that he could do and that he should return to his post in Sikkim. Since the Chinese now had a semi-permanent mission there seemed no good reason why we should let them continue to hold the fort. Gould at his final meeting with the Cabinet raised some complicated point that could not be settled immediately, and when this was pointed out he simply informed them that Hugh Richardson would be staying on to deal with any outstanding matters. The Chinese didn't go and we didn't go. It was as simple as that."

SOURCES

This chapter is mostly compiled from *Lhasa, The Holy City*, by F. Spencer Chapman. My thanks to Chatto and Windus and the Hogarth Press for their permission to quote from this book.

'Kate', Tsarong's daughter, married to the son of the noble family of Shatra

The Potala from the east . . .

CHAPTER EIGHT

Staying on in Lhasa

As he watched his colleagues set out on the long trek back to India, it was, for Hugh Richardson, the beginning of a long connection with Tibet.

"**N**OBODY had been in Lhasa for so long and I had to find out who was important and who was friendly. In fact they were all very friendly. I also had to get to know how the Tibetans thought and how they lived.

"When one first arrived in Tibet one had a sense of wonderment and excitement which then gave way to an understanding that one was living in a very well-ordered society. Lhasa was really the heart and soul of Tibet. It was

medieval and, in a way, deliberately underdeveloped – materially. Spiritually, however, and in general intelligence, it was highly developed.

"I think we had known before we went to Lhasa that everybody who had been there before had found the Tibetans very good company indeed, very hospitable and well-mannered. The Dekyi-Lingka was really not much more than a small summerhouse and we could not do much entertaining in it; but we had a fine garden and we used to have large garden parties. It was the main way of meeting people in easy, relaxed surroundings. Officials came with their wives and their children and we had immensely long, quite hilarious meals and then played very simple and relaxed games. All, from the abbots of the great monasteries and the Cabinet Ministers to the minor monk officials and minor lay officials, were very happy to take part in them, to shoot at a target with a .22 air rifle or play bowls. We had a cinema where we used to show films. Charlie Chaplin was a tremendous hit and never failed to cause an uproar of shouts and laughter. It was not only entertainment; it was a chance to make many friends and pick up a great deal of information.

Lhasa from the south

The Sakya Lama and his family in the garden of the Dekyi-Lingka

The Sakya Lama and his wife

Hugh Richardson at the Chumpithang dak bungalow between the Nathu-la Pass and Yatung

Dr. Guthrie entering the Dekyi-Lingka with the Sakya Lama

Dangtopa, a Lhasa official wearing the ceremonial dress
called Gyaluche

Four Tsipons (finance directors), Namseling,
Lukhang, Ngapho and Shakabpa

(*right*) Jigme Taring in official dress

The Dekyi-Lingka garden

"In the conduct of official business in Tibet there was rarely ever any sense of urgency. Discussions were long, calm and deliberate. Traditional and ancient civil and religious rites were just as much a part of the business of government as regular duties and administration. Whole days were devoted to such ceremonies, attendance at which was obligatory. It was all far from mere pageantry; it was considered a vital necessity for the welfare of the state.

"Official holidays were occasions of informal ceremony. For a week or more in the autumn, all government business was interrupted and the population of Lhasa repaired to the parks surrounding the city where each department of the government gave an all-day party, while the ordinary folk held their own merrymaking under the trees.

"Although Tibetans played at being very simple people, one should not have been taken in by that for very long. It was a game they had been at for 1300 years. They were shrewd diplomatic operators, but their religion dominated their every thought and action. 'Church' and 'State' were almost interchangeable terms.

Civil servants competing in
a compulsory archery competition

The Regent's annual sermon
to the monks in Lhasa, on the
15th day of the 1st month,
expounding the reason for The
Great Prayer

"Almost every family supplied at least one son to the monasteries. It was considered a matter of pride and prestige. It was not so much a vocation to join the priesthood; rather it was part of the social fabric of the country. They might enter a monastery at the age of five or six, and would be trained to read and write and to memorise religious texts, and a very important activity was debating religious problems of great complexity. They would meet in little parks attached to the monastery and spend hours in a rather formalised form of debating and discussion. If a boy passed his examinations he would be admitted to a college and, after taking certain vows, become a novice and be allowed to wear the red robes of the priesthood. After this there were various examinations to be passed, each opening the door to successive well-defined positions.

"Not all the monks, however, followed a career of learning. At an early stage they could choose a life suited to their special aptitude, for the larger monasteries were like medieval cities. They were a community with cooks and sweepers and administrators and police and musicians and those who were skilled in ritual. Others, presumably those who found that they were unsuited to a life of contemplation and learning, worked on the monastery estates or at trade. Tibetans are born traders.

"The years following the death of the 13th Dalai Lama, the late thirties, were, within Tibet, particularly quiet. But in the world outside things were happening that were eventually going to have a decisive influence on Tibet's future.

"In China there was civil war between the Nationalists and the Communists. Then, in June 1937, war between China and Japan broke out. The Chinese, who had been pressing on with their plans to send the Panchen Lama back with an armed escort, could not afford to have a war with Tibet as well. Then, to the mingled sorrow and relief of the Tibetan people, that gentle, hapless, troubled figure temporarily solved the problem by 'withdrawing to The Heavenly Field'. Tibet was now without both its spiritual leaders.

"The Tibetan Government at this time was totally preoccupied with the search for the new incarnation of the Dalai Lama. When the 13th Dalai Lama was embalmed his face was found to have turned towards the north-east and rainbows were seen in that direction. The Regent visited a holy, prophetic lake to the north of Lhasa and saw in it the letter 'A'. Together these and many other signs were taken to mean that the rebirth would be in the province of Am-do in north-eastern Tibet. Accordingly, district officials were instructed to be on the alert for news of the birth of any remarkable boy and of any marvellous signs in connection with his birth. Search parties were sent out. They were to look for a three-storeyed monastery with gilded roof and

Entering a monastery at the age of five or six,
they would meet in little parks attached to the
monastery and memorise religious texts.

turquoise tiles, and, nearby, a small house with unusual eaves. The Regent had seen a vision of this reflected in the waters of the lake. Here it was thought the child would be found. For two years they searched.

"Then, in the summer of 1938, a search party, disguised in the clothes of their servants, found a small boy playing in a house similar to that described by the Regent. The boy immediately saw through the disguise of the lamas and he quickly distinguished between the various articles that had belonged to the 13th Dalai Lama and the exact copies with which the search parties had also been provided. They knew immediately that they had discovered the 14th incarnation of the Dalai Lama. But they were far away from Lhasa, near the great monastery of Kum Bum in north-east Tibet, in an area under Chinese control.

"The problem facing Tibetans was how they could get him back to Lhasa without the return of Chinese political influence; over this there were prolonged negotiations. Eventually the Tibetan Government had to ransom him from the provincial governor who was virtually independent of the central government of China. We provided the Tibetans with a lot of silver, on easy terms, so that they could pay the ransom and, in October 1939, he was brought with his family to Lhasa.

The great tented camp below Rikya monastery

"There was tremendous excitement about his coming. A special party headed by a Cabinet Minister went out to meet him some ten days' short of Lhasa, acknowledge him as Dalai Lama and bring him in in state in the Dalai Lama's golden palanquin. I went out on the day, October 6, 1939, very early and we all waited. The whole population of Lhasa, so it seemed, had congregated in bright, cool autumn weather on the plain below Rikya monastery, some two miles from Lhasa. There a great camp sheltered the Peacock Tent. The front was open. In the centre stood the tall throne of the Dalai Lama, covered in patterned gold and red brocade. There was a lower throne at one side for the Regent. The band of the Dalai Lama's bodyguard was heard in the distance; and soon in a cloud of dust and of incense smoke from burners all along the route, the first banners of the procession appeared. Long trumpets sounded from the monastery above and the crowd pressed forward. A small troop of Chinese soldiers in dusty, quilted uniforms came first, at a quick pace, and then a long line of mounted men, carriers of banners and symbols, and then the whole body of Tibetan officials in ascending order of importance in magnificent brocades. At last in the centre of the cavalcade we saw a small carrying chair draped in yellow silk, and through the glass window the face of the little Dalai Lama could be seen looking calmly but

The view from the monastery

curiously at the mass of people prostrating themselves by the roadside, many weeping with joy. He was a very small boy, under five when he arrived. The procession moved at a rapid pace up the hill to the monastery where the child was to have a short rest and change his clothes. Soon he was carried down the winding path in the large gilded state palanquin with eight bearers in yellow silk and red tasselled hats. The whole official body accompanied him into the camp to the Peacock Tent where he was lifted onto the throne by his Lord Chamberlain. We were led to our seats, just in front of the Dalai Lama's family.

"The child, wearing yellow brocade and a yellow, peaked hat with a fur brim sat quietly and with great dignity, completely at ease in these strange surroundings, giving the proper blessing to each person, according to their rank. It took a very long time. When our turn came to offer our scarves he was smiling broadly and as I bent down for his blessing he took a pull at my hair. For an hour the stream of worshippers continued to flow until at last he was lifted down and carried back up to the monastery.

The tall throne of the Dalai Lama

"Two days later he was brought in state into Lhasa. In the Jo-Khang he was initiated as a monk and assumed names which mean 'The Holy One, The Gentle Glory, Powerful in Speech, Pure in Mind, Holder of the Faith, Ocean of Wisdom'. He behaved with the most superb composure and immediately won the devotion of his people by his charm and self-possession. They constantly noted his similarities with the late Dalai Lama – his special kindness to the latter's servants, and his love of music and flowers. They were deeply moved to have him back.

"The formal installation in the Potala did not take place until early the following year when Sir Basil Gould came up from India on a special mission and with proper presents for the occasion; a pedal car, a tricycle, a cuckoo clock and a musical box.

"The Dalai Lama in theory assumes absolute power at the age of about 18, but in practice certain checks will ensure that he conforms to the ancient customs of the country. In the first place, though he is the apex and the glory of the system, it is to the system that he owes his position. Then he will be brought up exclusively by learned and influential monks and lamas. A further check on the power of Dalai Lamas is that the office cannot be hereditary and the method of selection is such that the child is usually found in a simple family; thereafter his relations, though ennobled, are excluded from taking part in the administration."

'They were deeply moved
to have him back.'

The Dalai Lama's mother and
brothers and sisters

The procession to the formal installation . . .

"To the outside world Tibetan life may appear backward and the Tibetan Government a repository of curiously slow-moving and archaic customs; but a civilisation and a government deserve to be seen in a proper perspective and judged by their results. Simplicity and deliberateness are not the same thing as stupidity and inefficiency, nor are ancient customs and institutions necessarily bad. The Tibetans are easy-going, kindly, cheerful and contented. The people are not downtrodden, oppressed or exploited. In 13 centuries of recorded history there is no mention of popular discontent against the government. The Tibetans accept their long-established way of life and their social inequalities with active contentment. That may seem surprising, even reprehensible, to those who are unable to value or tolerate the ideas and standards of other people and who long to level out all variety by the diffusion of material benefits which they take to be synonymous with progress. The Tibetans value the right, enjoyed in other countries, to progress in their own way."

SOURCES

This chapter is compiled from an interview with Hugh Richardson and from his writings. The account of the search for the Dalai Lama on pages 125–6 is derived from Sir Basil Gould's *The Jewel in the Lotus*. My thanks to Chatto and Windus for permission to quote from this book.

133   Monks at the New Year ceremonies

CHAPTER NINE

Tremors from the World Outside

War between China and Japan had broken out in June 1937. The Tibetans had a certain sympathy for China, compounded of an old feeling of esteem for Chinese civilisation, the dislike of any injustice and oppression – as inculcated by the Tibetan religion – and the thought that the Chinese were too occupied with the war to be of much trouble to them. Moreover, the anxiety caused by the threat of the forced return of the Panchen Lama was gone. The Tibetans offered prayers for Chinese success but stayed strictly neutral.

In 1941 Japan entered the Second World War. The Tibetans decided that it would be in their best interests to remain neutral; they adamantly refused to permit the transit of war supplies across Tibet from India to China.

The war also created a new alliance between Britain and China. The Tibetans found themselves under pressure from the British Government to make concessions to the Chinese and were gravely disconcerted. The prayers which they offered were not for the allied cause but, in general terms, for the restoration of peace. Relations between China and Tibet again became acutely embittered.

Hugh Richardson had left Tibet in 1940, posted as Secretary at the British Mission in Chungking, seat of the Chinese Government. In 1944 he was back in Lhasa.

In 1940 a young Austrian mountaineer, Heinrich Harrer, who had been on a climbing expedition in India when the Second World War broke out, was interned by the British in a camp near Dehra Dun. He looked up longingly at the sunlit, lonely heights of the Himalayas and plotted his escape. By June 1944 he and his friend Peter Aufschnaiter were free, furtively clambering their way up the Himalayan passes towards Tibet. Tibet then was still a closed country, forbidden to all foreigners save those few political representatives, British and Chinese, warily countering each other's influence on the fringes of their respective empires, but now in common cause against the Japanese.

At the same time a new Chinese representative, Dr. Tsung-lien Shen, was on his way to Lhasa. He was educated at Harvard and at the Sorbonne, and afterwards had been a professor of history at various universities in China. He

was an able, unostentatious and broadminded man, an advisor of Chiang Kai-shek, and very much a patriot. He thought of the Tibetans as one of the 'five races of China' and on historical grounds he considered China's claims to Tibet were strong.

"I was charged to strengthen the ties between China and Tibet and to keep open the caravan route to war-torn China. Since 1911, Lhasa has to all practical purposes enjoyed full independence. It has its own currency and customs; it runs its own telegraph and postal services; it maintains a civil service different from that of any other part of China and it even keeps its own army. In policy Lhasa often acts even more independently. Lhasa believes that to be attached politically to China is more a liability than an asset.

A nomad family

"But China and Tibet for many hundreds of years have been bound by a spiritual and earthly connection – the Buddhist religion of Tibet guarded by the aid and protection of China – a relationship that has been weakened by wars and revolutions in China.

"I went to Lhasa by way of India and Sikkim, where I stayed with Mr. Basil Gould at the British Residency before crossing the Himalayas to Tibet. Tibet from the earliest times has been the subject of the most extravagant stories and myths but the moment you set foot in Tibet, you wonder, 'Can this be Shangri-La, the promised wonderland?' It is bleak and barren, wrapped in silence. When you draw near the heart of the hermit kingdom, you begin to experience moments of difficult mental adjustment. You realise that you are heading into a society fossilised many centuries back, and that you are supposed to behave there like one of its members. Now as you approach the centre of Tibetan civilisation, everything hardens into the mould of a harsh tradition that dictates what you must do and what you must not, and turns all your social contacts into dry, dead formalities."

The British Residency, Sikkim   136

Outside Lhasa, Shen was welcomed by members of the Chinese community and by Jigme Taring, now an official at the Finance Ministry, representing the Tibetan Government. Then, preceded by a Tibetan band, Shen and his staff rode on into Lhasa, the Guomintang flag at their head, fluttering in the breeze.

Shen was a diplomat of the old school. Despite his initial reaction to Tibet, he made many friends and won a higher degree of Tibetan confidence than any of his predecessors but he had many difficulties to weather. The Tibetans continued to be worried about Chinese intentions. One of the former Panchen Lama's staff, who was also a member of the Chinese Central Executive Committee, announced that the reincarnation of the Panchen Lama had been found in China, and had been acknowledged and enthroned in that office. The Tibetan Government did not recognise him but once again the Chinese had a pretender in their hands.

'. . . welcomed by Jigme Taring, representing the Tibetan Government'

'The Guomintang flag at their head . . .'

Heinrich Harrer and Peter Aufschnaiter succeeded in making it to the Tibetan border.

"AT the top of a high pass were heaps of stones and prayerflags. It was very cold. As far as the eye could see there were only empty mountain heights and deserted valleys.

"For nearly two years we wandered, skirting distant villages, passing ourselves off as pilgrims. Sometimes we journeyed in the company of caravans but mostly alone, alternately shunned by suspicious nomads or welcomed into their black felt tents. Many nights we spent in inhospitable depressions in the ground, barely shielded from the wind.

"In the winter we crossed the wild barren Chang-Tang, through the loneliest landscape I had ever seen – a sea of snowy mountains.

"Lhasa! The very name had always given us a thrill. On our painful marches and during icy nights, we had clung to it and drawn new strength from it. No pilgrim from the most distant province could ever have yearned for the Holy City more than we did.

"So ragged and tattered were we that we looked more like brigands from the Chang-Tang than Europeans.

"It was January 15, 1946 when we set out on our last march and entered the broad valley of the Kyi-Chu. We turned a corner and saw, gleaming in the distance, the golden roofs of the Potala. We felt inclined to go down on our knees like the pilgrims do. We had covered over 600 miles with the vision of this fabulous, forbidden city forever in our minds.

"It was late in the afternoon when we reached the great western gate of the city. We just walked through together with all the other pilgrims, with the merchants, with farmers, with caravans and donkeys bringing loads into Lhasa.

"Nobody stopped us or bothered us. We realised that no one, not even a European, was suspect because no one had ever before come to Lhasa without a pass. To this day I can find no words to express how overwhelming were our sensations. The setting sun bathed the golden spires of the Jo-Khang Cathedral in an unearthly light. Shivering with cold, we looked for lodgings.

"A crowd gathered round us. They saw our open, blistered feet and brought us some food. Suddenly we heard ourselves addressed in perfect English. We looked up, astonished; it was a richly-clad Tibetan who had spoken to us. He invited us into his house.

"We were in Lhasa."

In the central marketplace

This chapter is compiled from various sources; page 134 from Hugh Richardson's *Tibet and Its History*; page 135, last paragraph, from Sir Basil Gould's *The Jewel in the Lotus*; pages 135–6 from Dr. Shen Tsung-lien's *Tibet and the Tibetans* (my thanks to Stanford University Press for permission to quote from this book). Page 137 is from Hugh Richardson *op. cit.*; page 138 from Heinrich Harrer's *Seven Years in Tibet*.

In front of the Potala

CHAPTER TEN

The Last Days of the Old Tibet

"OUR host, Thangme, was a fifth rank official in charge of the electricity plant. He visited the Foreign Minister and brought word that, for the time being, we might stay in Lhasa. We were afraid that we might be sent back to internment in India.

"It is probable that no country in the world would welcome two poor fugitives as Tibet welcomed us. We were the talk of the town. Everyone wanted to see us and hear the story of our adventures. The Tibetans are proud of their organisation for keeping out foreigners and they found the manner in which we had broken through the barriers highly amusing.

"A parcel of clothes, a gift from the government, arrived with apologies for the delay, caused by the fact that we were taller than the average Tibetan and there were no ready-made clothes to fit us. The son of the celebrated Minister Tsarong came with his wife, Yangchenla. She was not at all shy, but questioned us in a lively manner about our journey and broke into our explanations with bursts of laughter. Our friends later told us that we spoke Tibetan with the commonest kind of peasant dialect.

"For the first week we were kept indoors. It was a great surprise when one day we were invited to visit the Dalai Lama's parents. Our hosts gave us white scarves and hurried us on our way. Such an invitation overrode everything. We were led through a large garden full of vegetable plots and willows, and taken up to the first floor of the house. A door was opened and we found ourselves in the presence of the mother of the God-King. She was sitting on a small throne in a large, bright room surrounded by servants. She smiled at us and we bowed and handed her the white scarves. The father of the Dalai Lama came in, a dignified, elderly man. He shook hands most unaffectedly and contrary to Tibetan custom. Then we all sat down to tea. They had lived as simple peasants till their son was recognised as the incarnation of the Dalai Lama. Three of their six children had been recognised as incarnations.

"Loaded with presents and escorted by servants we returned to Thangme's house. Our hosts waited for us with impatient excitement and we had to tell them every detail; the Tibetans feel a humble awe for The Great Mother.

"Ten days after our arrival we received word from the Foreign Ministry that we could move about the town freely while they decided what should be done with us.

"We paid visits to the Cabinet Ministers and senior monk officials to do whatever we could to convince them we were harmless. We called on the youngest minister first. Surkhang was 32 and was considered more progressive than his colleagues. He welcomed us with frank cordiality and we were immediately on good terms. He was astonishingly well-informed about events in the outside world. He entertained us to a princely dinner and when we took our leave we felt that we had known each other for years.

"The monk minister received us with less formality than the others. In a general way he seemed detached and avoided expressing definite opinions as had the others. The political situation in the world outside Tibet must have been causing him anxiety.

"For three weeks we enjoyed Thangme's hospitality. He had taken us in as vagabonds and had been a true friend to us.

"Now Tsarong invited us to stay. Tsarong was an extraordinary man, a self-made man of the most modern brand. He had consistently endeavoured to introduce reforms and whenever the government were busy with an important problem he was called in to advise. His was a large house with a beautiful garden."

"It was spring. March had come and on the 4th of the month began the new year festival, called The Great Prayer. I was confined to bed with sciatica but in the distance I could hear drums and horns, and saw by the excitement in the house how important it all was.

'The abbots descend into the town like conquerors . . .'

Monks in the streets of Lhasa

A monk policeman

Tsarong's House

The city magistrates hand over authority to the abbots.

"The abbots in their finest garments and the 20,000 monks from the monasteries around Lhasa descend into the town like conquerors, doubling its population, for the three weeks of the ceremonies. The city magistrates hand over authority to the monks, symbolising the restoration by the secular power of its office to religion, to whom it originally belonged. This is the beginning of a strict and formidable regime. The whole town is tidied up and crimes and offences, particularly gambling, are punished with especial severity.

"By the 15th of the first Tibetan month I was so much better that I could attend the festivities. Tens of thousands of people had flocked into the town and Lhasa looked like a great encampment. On the 15th we watched a magnificent procession in the Barkhor, the central street of Lhasa. We sat with Mrs. Tsarong at the ground-floor window of a house they owned. Strange, framelike objects were erected in the street. Soon after sunset gaily coloured butter sculptures made by the different monasteries were attached to them. In front was an endless mass of people. It began to grow dark. The Lhasa regiments marched up to the sound of trumpets and drums and lined the streets. The whole scene was lit by thousands of butter lamps. The voices of the crowd were hushed in anticipation. The great moment had come. The cathedral doors opened and the young God-King stepped slowly out, supported to right and left by two abbots. The people bowed in awe as the Dalai Lama began his solemn circuit of the Barkhor. From time to time he stopped before the figures of butter and gazed at them. He was followed by all the high dignatories and nobles. Only the music of the monks could be heard – the oboes, tubas and kettledrums. It was like a vision of another world. In the yellow light of the flickering lamps, the great figures of moulded butter seemed to come to life. Now the Living Buddha was approaching. The crowd was frozen. Soon the Dalai Lama had completed his tour and vanished into the Jo-Khang. As if woken from a hypnotic sleep the tens of thousands of spectators broke into chaos.

'The twenty thousand monks . . .'   144

"Next morning the streets were empty. As if to emphasise the Buddhist theme that all life is transitory and has no more substance than dreams, the butter sculptures had vanished."

'On the 15th of the month . . .'

"For six days in succession, from the 22nd of the month, there is a spectacle every day. Two lay officials are appointed commanders of an army of 1,000 medieval soldiers. Long ago a Moslem army marching on Lhasa was overtaken by a heavy snowstorm and perished. Their arms and armour were brought in triumph to Lhasa and now are brought out every year; one hears the clink of chain mail on men and horses; helmets bearing Arabic inscriptions reflect the sunshine; reports of the old muzzle-loaders echo in the narrow streets. The commanders lead the army to a great review on the plains to the north of Lhasa.

'The commanders of the army . . .'

A commander and his attendants

'Maids of Honour' before the parade

'An army of 1000 medieval soldiers . . .'

The commanders preparing to ride off
to the great parade

"The next morning the cavalry, reinforced by hundreds of foot soldiers, also in armour and with helmets bedecked with flags and plumes, wage a phantom war against the enemies of Buddhism. They literally blast their way into Lhasa, firing their guns at every step and making a terrific din. At the entrance to the Jo-Khang the commanders prostrate themselves before the Dalai Lama. Inside two services, for the chastisement of evil spirits, are being held. The service completed, two columns of monks escort an effigy of a skull symbolising evil and proceed through the town.

'Riding off to wage their phantom war . . .'

The cavalry

'Literally blasting their way
into Lhasa . . .'

A detachment of the feudal militia

'An effigy of a skull symbolising evil . . .'

"Then the Oracle of Nechung, the State Oracle, wearing a huge, feathered headdress and supported by two monks, is brought running from the Jo-Khang. Before a vast gathering of monks in front of the Potala, the Oracle, trembling and shaking in a trance, predicts specific events for the year to come. His trance over, he is borne away in a palanquin while the monks light two vast brushwood pyres on which the effigy is ceremonially burnt. The two commanders and their 1,000 knights then converge on the scene of the pyres. The enemies of Buddhism finally defeated, they return with shouts and cheers to Lhasa to spread the good news.

'The oracle of Nechung is brought running from the Jo-Khang.'

Wrestling bouts

Weight-lifting

'The monks disperse to their monasteries.'

"The celebrations continue with an athletic gathering on the Barkhor. We watch it from the second floor of the Chinese Legation, as guests of Dr. Shen. Every vantage point is crammed with spectators; officials in their silk brocades, monks and pilgrims. The first events are wrestling bouts that have no particular rules. There is no distinction between winners and losers. Both get a reward.

"Next comes a weightlifting competition. The weight is a heavy, smooth stone which must have seen hundreds of New Year festivals. There is much laughter when a competitor swaggers up to the stone with an air of confidence and then finds that he can hardly lift it off the ground. Then there are running races and riderless horse races which are followed with tremendous excitement.

"When the celebration is over the monks disperse to their monasteries, leaving Lhasa once more to its old order.

'At the test of horsemanship . . .'

'This manifestation of their faith . . .'

"The lay festivities last two more days, the most popular spectacle being a test of horsemanship held outside Lhasa on the plain. Here tents draped with silks and brocades are pitched in serried ranks. Men dressed in ancient armour gallop past a hanging target, swing up their matchlocks and shoot into the bullseye. Before they reach the next target 20 yards away they have exchanged their matchlocks for bows and arrows. Every noble family has to enter a certain number of participants. It is probably a survival of former great military parades when feudal lords had to march their troops past their overlord and thus show their readiness for war. At the end of the festival the nobles march back to the town in a glittering procession. Workaday life begins again. Shops reopen, dice-players appear at street corners, and the dogs, who had migrated to the outskirts, come back into town."

"Summer approached and nothing was said about our expulsion. Aufschnaiter, who was trained as an agricultural engineer, was summoned by a high monastic official and commissioned to build an irrigation canal. I earned my keep by giving lessons in mathematics and English. We were feeling settled in Lhasa. Europe with its life of turmoil seemed far away.

"I was soon earning enough to rent a house of my own. I built a tennis court. Mr. Lieu, secretary to Mr. Shen at the Chinese Legation, was incontestably the best player. Then came Mr. Richardson, the British representative, a gaunt Scotsman, slim and tough in his professional work and one of the greatest experts on Tibet's past.

"Every year, after consideration of the omens, a day is fixed on which the summer season is officially declared to have begun, and whatever the weather, the nobles and monks must then leave off their winter furs and put on summer dress. At this time all the officials accompany the Dalai Lama in a great procession from the Potala to the Norbu-Lingka.

"The whole town moved out to watch. First came servants with the God-King's personal effects. At intervals behind rode monks with banners decorated with texts; then high dignatories and abbots of the God-King's household; and then the palanquin of the Living Buddha, gleaming gold in the sunlight. All heads were bowed as the band played 'God Save the King,' the British national anthem which was also the national anthem of Tibet; the Lhasa bandmaster had been trained in India.

"Pilgrims from the remotest parts of Tibet would undergo countless hardships in order to witness once in their lives this brilliant manifestation of their faith, and they feed on the memory during their hard and lonely lives. We could not close our hearts to the religious fervour that radiated from everyone.

"Religion is the heart and fabric of the state. In all my years in Tibet I never met anyone who expressed the slightest doubt about Lord Buddha's teaching. After a short time in the country it was impossible for me to kill a fly. All living things are sacred. Later when I was in charge of earthworks, I used to see how

the coolies would go through each spadeful and take out the worms to put them in a safe place. It follows that there is no capital punishment in Tibet. Murderers are flogged and fettered. Theft and various minor crimes are punished with public whippings and the pillory. Here charitable people come and give them food and drink.

"The Tibetan calendar is based on the cycles of the moon. The day of the full moon is the 15th of the month and of the new moon, the 30th. Certain dates which are deemed auspicious are duplicated; others, deemed inauspicious, are omitted. Thus you may find February 2 twice in succession and no date between February 3 and February 5. The Tibetans are a superstitious people. One does not do a thing without consulting the omens.

"The 4th month of the year is Holy Month – the month in which Lord Buddha was born. Special prayers are organised throughout the city and lamps lit before every altar. From the first day men and women, rich and poor, walk the Lingkhor, the Holy Walk around Lhasa. It is the most popular way to gain merit. Some sit beside running streams dipping images of Buddha into the current. On the 15th of the month the government officials, in their brilliant silk costumes, are led by the four Cabinet Ministers around the Lingkhor.

Walking the Lingkhor

Dipping images of Buddha into the water

Prayer charms and incense smoke on the Lingkhor

The procession to the Norbu-Lingka

155

The Government Officials, led by the Cabinet Ministers

"Later the same day there is a beautiful and informal festival at the Dragon Temple, on an island in a lake behind the Potala. There is a holiday atmosphere. Wine and food shops spring up, picnic parties are everywhere. The ministers preside over a small ceremony in the Temple. Afterwards they are rowed around the island in hide boats and they sink five treasures into the lake as a dedication to the gods.

'At the Dragon Temple . . .'

'The flower show . . .'

'They put up tents . . .'

"The picnic season had come. Throughout the summer the citified people of Lhasa flock to the parks by the river. Recalling the traditions of their nomadic forbears, they put up tents and organise parties. Many young women who have studied in India proudly display their modern bathing suits. In the intervals of splashing about in the water, the bathers picnic and play games with much laughter, and in the evening every party burns incense by the riverside in gratitude to the gods for a lovely day. When the sun is down and the moon is up, the greater part of the revelling public pour back into the

town, boisterous and merry. Men and women, arm in arm, walk on unsteady legs, singing and laughing like children.

"The 7th month is the time of Opera. Vast throngs of people come to see a flower show and dramatic performances given on a great stone stage in the garden of the Norbu-Lingka. It goes on for seven days from sunrise to sunset. I could not but be astonished at the frankness of some of the performances. It is proof of the good humour and sanity of the people that they can make fun of their own weaknesses and even of their religious institutions. Men appear dressed as nuns and even go so far as to give a performance of the Oracle, with dance, trance and all. It brings the house down. When monks and nuns begin to flirt together on the stage, no one can stop laughing and tears roll down the cheeks of even the sternest abbots in the audience. The Dalai Lama witnesses these performances from behind a gauze curtain at a window in the first floor of a pavilion overlooking the stage. When the drama week is over the actors are invited to play in the houses of noblemen and in the monasteries. The performances are besieged by the public and the police often have to intervene to keep order.

'Dramatic performances . . .

"As the warm months pass and the trees begin to shed their leaves and the meadows show the first tinges of brown, the people of Tibet begin to whitewash their houses, white being the colour of prosperity. In Lhasa the signal is given by the Potala where buckets full of limewash are dashed over its white façade.

The Potala and the village of Sho

"In the autumn, with pomp and circumstance, the Dalai Lama returns to the Potala. Splendid and impressive as the Potala is, it is miserably dark and uncomfortable as a dwelling place. I had several opportunities of staying in the Potala as the guest of a monk friend. Life in this religious fortress resembles, one supposes, that of a medieval castle. Hardly an object belongs to the present day. In the evening all the gates are closed under the supervision of the Treasurer, after which watchmen go through the whole palace to see that everything is in order. Their shouts ringing along the corridors are the only sound in the oppressive stillness. The nights are long and peaceful. Everyone goes to bed early. In contrast to the brisk social life in the city there are no parties or entertainments. From the shrines of the Holy Dead emanates an atmosphere of mortality, dim and solemn, which makes the whole palace feel like an enormous tomb. I felt sorry for the Child-God isolated in that dark and gloomy fortress, while in the city below other children were enjoying themselves.

Returning to the Potala

'While other children were enjoying themselves . . .'
(sliding on a frozen pool below the Potala)

The Dalai Lama, a boy of 14

"Just before our second Tibetan New Year in Lhasa we received our first letters from home in three years. The news from Europe was not encouraging. It strengthened our desire to make a permanent home in Lhasa. The time we had spent there had had a formative effect on our characters. I used to listen to the world news on the wireless and shake my head at the things which men seemed to think important. Here it is the yak's pace which dictates the tempo of life, and so it has been for 1,000 years. The Chinese invented the wheel 2,000 years ago but the Tibetans will have none of it. Here they still believe that the world is flat. But would Tibet be happier for being transformed? It might rob the people of their peace and leisure.

"One day riding home from work I was overtaken by an excited soldier of the bodyguard who told me that I must at once go to the Norbu-Lingka where I had been asked to build a small cinema. Before I could enter, the door opened and I was standing before the Dalai Lama. Conquering my surprise I bowed deeply. He beamed all over his face. He was a boy of 14 with a pale complexion and eyes full of expression. He wore the same red robes as the monk officials. He took a lively interest in how the projector worked and in a documentary I showed on the capitulation of Japan.

"About this time we began to feel the repercussions of world politics, even amidst the peace of Lhasa. In 1947 had come India's independence. Richardson, however, stayed on in Lhasa, as representative of the Indian Government, until 1950. Then the Civil War in China assumed more disquieting aspects. The Tibetans realised that the Chinese Communists would not tolerate their religion. The Chinese had already conquered Sikang and Turkestan in the north, and even the parts bordering eastern Tibet. In Peking it was solemnly declared that Tibet was the next to be 'liberated'.

"In July 1949 the Tibetan Government decided to expel the whole Chinese mission in Lhasa. They were treated with exquisite courtesy and invited to farewell parties, and accompanied out with a big band of musicians and with white scarves around their necks.

"The little Tibetan Army was hurriedly reorganised under the supervision of a Cabinet Minister. Monks and officials were trained as officers. New regiments were raised and the richer classes called upon to furnish and equip another 1,000 men.

The little Tibetan army

'New regiments were raised.'

◄ The whole Chinese mission was expelled

'New colours were inaugurated . . .'

"Not only were the material means of defence mobilised but also the spiritual forces of the people. All the monks in Tibet were ordered to attend public services. New prayerflags and prayerwheels were set up everywhere. Offerings were doubled and on the mountains incense fires burned. The people believed with rocklike faith that the power of religion would suffice to protect their independence. Meanwhile Radio Peking was sending out messages in Tibetan promising that Tibet would soon be 'freed'.

"As the threat of 'liberation' grew nearer, more people than ever streamed to the religious festivals which, in the early days of 1950, surpassed in pomp and splendour anything I had ever seen. It seemed that the entire population of Tibet had gathered in pious enthusiasm in the narrow streets of Lhasa. Despite the threat from the Chinese, the ceremonies vital to the running of the state had to continue. Once more I watched the great parade of ancient cavalry on the plain behind the Potala. It was held each year in front of the house where in 1904 Younghusband had stayed. Then he and his mission were the first Europeans of the time to see Lhasa. I did not know it at the time but I, 45 years later, was to be the last European to see the old Tibet.

"Four weeks after the great New Year Festival the 20,000 monks of the monasteries round Lhasa descended once again into the city for the Second Prayer Festival. The full force of the Tantric order was mobilised. In front of the central cathedral the abbots of the great monasteries were challenged to throw dice to decide the fate of Tibet. Two scapegoats symbolising evil were the challengers. These demons with their faces painted half white and half black and dressed in sheepskins advanced to the Jo-Khang shouting on all the devils to come and witness their gamble with Tibet. Representatives of the Tibetan Government supervised the contest. They took no chances. The dice were loaded, the faces of the abbots' dice all marked with sixes, those of the demons with ones.

'The abbots of the great monasteries . . .'

"The moment ritual victory was won for Tibet, the scapegoats were driven from the town taking with them all the potential misfortunes of the year to come. The prayers ended with a procession symbolising the dedication of his subjects to the Dalai Lama.

The mile-long procession
to the foot of the Potala

The procession leaving the Jo-Khang

"When the head of the mile-long procession reached the Potala a huge silk banner of the Buddha was lowered from the face of the Potala. The New Year appropriately and successfully observed, the people of Lhasa would, in normal times, relax and agree that they had good reason to look forward to another year of peace and prosperity.

'. . . a huge silk banner of the Buddha
was lowered from the face of the Potala'

'The State Oracle was frequently consulted.'

"But this year the prayers failed, as did the game of dice. Evil omens multiplied. Monsters were born. In August there was an earthquake; the houses of Lhasa began to shake and a distant rumbling could be heard. In vain the government sent monks to the centres of ill omen to banish the evil spirits. The town buzzed with rumours. The State Oracle was frequently consulted. His prophecies were dark. 'A powerful foe threatens our sacred land from north and east. Our religion is in danger.'

"With the approach of autumn came news that the Chinese were massing troops on the frontier. The Dalai Lama, just 15 years old, was hurriedly declared of age. The old Regent stepped down.

"On October 7, 1950, the enemy attacked the Tibetan frontier in six places simultaneously. The National Assembly appealed to the United Nations for help. The appeal was rejected, with the UN expressing the hope that China and Tibet would come to a peaceful agreement. The people waited for a miracle. Then came the news of the first defeats. The government sent for all the most famous oracles in Tibet. There were dramatic scenes in the Norbu-Lingka. The grey-haired abbots and veteran ministers entreated the oracles to stand by them in their hour of need. Should the Dalai Lama stay or flee? The Tibetan Government could not make such an important decision; the gods must have the last word. The State Oracle said 'flee.'

"The Dalai Lama's flight was kept strictly secret. For the last time the high officials drank butter tea in the Potala, and then their cups were refilled and left standing as a charm to bring about a speedy return.

"They headed southwards across the Tsang-po river along the old trade route to India. News of the Dalai Lama's approach soon reached Gyantse. Small white stones were laid along the sides of the streets to ward off evil

Approaching Gyantse

'Incense fires burned in welcome.'   172

'They headed southwards . . .'
(the gorge between Phari Dzong
and the Chumbi Valley)

173

spirits. Incense fires burned in welcome. Monks and nuns flocked from the monasteries and convents, and the whole population waited for hours to receive their King and beg him not to leave them.

"From Gyantse the party carried on across the Himalayas. Sixteen days after leaving Lhasa the caravan halted in the Chumbi valley on the borders of India.

"I stayed with his Holiness in the Chumbi Valley for three more months, still believing that we might be able to return, but I soon realised that it was the end of the old Tibet.

The Dalai Lama crossing the Tsang-po

Arriving in the Chumbi Valley

Chinese troops entering Lhasa

"I had escaped from the British into Tibet. For five happy years I had lived in Lhasa and it was the last place on earth you would ever have thought you would have to escape from again. I could but hope that the Tibetans, whose only wish was to live in peace and freedom, would not have to suffer too much now that a communist regime was to rule their land.

"With a heavy heart I said goodbye to the Dalai Lama.

"Wherever I live I shall feel homesick for Tibet."

SOURCES

This chapter is mostly compiled from Heinrich Harrer's *Seven Years in Tibet*, but the descriptions of certain of the New Year and other ceremonies are filled out with material derived from Shen Tsung-lien's *Tibet and the Tibetans*, and from my observation of film shot by Shen and others in Lhasa in the 1940s.

Heinrich Harrer with a
Tibetan friend, Shokhang, during
the stay in the Chumbi Valley

CHAPTER ELEVEN

Behind the Bamboo Curtain

BY the beginning of 1951 the Chinese were well established in Tibet. They had swept aside the little Tibetan Army but did not push through to Lhasa. In contrast to their invasion of 1911, they made genuine efforts to appear conciliatory and co-operative. They released the Tibetan soldiers they'd captured and respected the monasteries. Messages were sent to the Dalai Lama in the Chumbi Valley in an effort to secure the peaceful 'liberation' of Tibet.

In May that year the first treaty between Tibet and China for more than 1,000 years was signed in Peking. Tibet was defined as being part of the Chinese Motherland. The Tibetans had no choice but to sign. The agreement pledged that there would be no change in the status and powers of the Dalai Lama and promised protection for the Tibetan religion.

In July the Dalai Lama returned to Lhasa. Outwardly life appeared to continue as it had before, dominated by the yearly cycle of religious festivals. But the Chinese tightened their hold on Tibet. There were soon many Chinese soldiers in Lhasa. Food and fuel became scarce. The Chinese found the Tibetans obstructive and unenthusiastic about Chinese ideas and ideology. This tried Chinese patience. They were derogatory about the existing system and tried to undermine the influence of the monasteries. They demanded the dismissal of certain government officials. The Tibetans in turn resented this interference. Relations between the Chinese and Tibetans deteriorated. Within less than a year there were signs of growing discontent amongst the common people.

In 1954 the Dalai Lama was invited on a long visit to Peking. The whole of Lhasa came out to see his Holiness's departure. Clouds of incense drifted over the Kyi-Chu river as the Dalai Lama and his party crossed in yak-hide coracles tied together. Vast crowds thronged the banks, weeping and praying for a safe journey and a quick return. The people were afraid that the Chinese would not let the Dalai Lama return.

It was an immense cavalcade that set off on ponies for Peking, hundreds of officials and monks with columns of servants, and baggage mules carrying

food and tents. Ahead went trumpeters and monks carrying the banners of the Dalai Lama. It was like a scene from the middle ages, recalling the visit to Peking of the 13th Dalai Lama, 45 years earlier. Then he was going to meet the Emperor; now it was to meet Chairman Mao.

For five months the Tibetans were in Peking, discussing the 'Unified Preparatory Committee for the Autonomous Region of Tibet'. In Peking there were many speeches about the great friendship between Tibetans and Chinese. In Lhasa the absence of the Dalai Lama caused anxiety and discontent but the people had kept quiet because the Dalai Lama was like a hostage in Peking.

January 1955: trucks arrive
from China on the newly
completed China–Tibet highway

177

After his return fighting broke out in eastern Tibet. New forms of taxation, attacks on the monasteries and the enforced redistribution of land had led to open discontent amongst the sturdy and independent Khampas. Then came a change in Chinese methods. Monasteries were destroyed by shelling and bombardment. Lamas were assaulted and humiliated. Eye-witnesses described to the International Commission of Jurists how monks and laymen were tortured and killed, women raped and others publicly humiliated, venerated lamas subjected to brutal and disgusting degradation, children taken from their homes, ostensibly for re-education in China, and sacred books, images and relics carried off or publicly destroyed.

In Lhasa tension and discontent grew further as the town became overcrowded with refugees and supplies became scarce. By late 1958 it was becoming obvious to disinterested observers that a serious explosion was about to take place. Armed guerrillas had taken control of the whole area to the south of the Tsang-po river. A Chinese military post only 25 miles from Lhasa was annihilated. Fighting continued in many eastern parts of Tibet. The Chinese brought in more and better troops.

In January 1959 the Chinese asked the Dalai Lama to go again to Peking. He declined, explaining that he had to undergo important religious examinations. Although he was already the ruler of Tibet he still had to prove that his religious knowledge made him worthy of the office. For three months he was to be questioned and examined at each of the three great monasteries of Lhasa. The Tibetan Government accompanied the Dalai Lama to the ceremonies and Cabinet meetings were held at the monasteries throughout the examinations. It must have infuriated the Chinese Communists, for whom all this kind of religious zeal was simply superstition, a tranquilising poison used by capitalists to suppress the people; even ten years after the Chinese takeover religion still dominated what was supposed to be part of an atheist People's Republic.

The Tibetan Government and the Dalai Lama had constantly striven for accommodation and compromise. They must have known that it was hopeless to oppose the might of China. There, the Revolution had grown out of the discontent of ordinary people. In Tibet it was ordinary people who were the main opponents of the Chinese.

In March 1959, shortly after the successful completion of his examinations the Dalai Lama was invited to attend a display at the Chinese barracks in Lhasa. The people thought this would be a trap; the Dalai Lama might be taken hostage; thousands, therefore, swarmed to the Norbu-Lingka to protect him. A Chinese emissary was stoned to death. The Tibetan people had taken matters into their own hands. They set up defensive positions

around the Norbu-Lingka. Tibetan soldiers and Khampas joined the defenders. The Dalai Lama strove desperately to reach a peaceful solution as he knew that open war with the Chinese would be disastrous.

The Chinese Military Area Command called an emergency meeting. 'Our patience finally exhausted,' it was stated, 'we resolved to suppress resolutely the rebellion and safeguard the unity and integrity of the Motherland.' The counterattack began; the Norbu-Lingka was bombarded. The Tibetans then turned on Chinese buildings and the barracks. Fighting flared all over Lhasa.

Unbeknownst to the Chinese the Dalai Lama had slipped out of the Norbu-Lingka by night. The last Tibetan Cabinet meeting had denounced all agreements with China on the grounds of persistent violations by China and had proclaimed Tibet independent.

The Chinese went on to inflict terrible losses on the Tibetans. Many thousands were killed or taken prisoner, among them Tsarong who had stayed behind in the Norbu-Lingka. Executions began. Thousands of men and boys were deported. The peace of desolation hung over Lhasa.

Many thousands were taken prisoner.

The Dalai Lama made good his escape. He and several thousand refugees eventually crossed the Himalayas into India to safety and an uncertain future. In India his arrival was greeted by a tremendous popular demonstration of world concern and relief, and by an embarrassed Indian Government. Nehru, afraid of provoking the Chinese, had preferred to pretend that nothing untoward was happening in Tibet.

The Chinese abolished the Tibetan Government and set up a military dictatorship using any Tibetan nobles or monastic officials who were willing to comply. Religious institutions came under immediate attack. The great monasteries of Lhasa were cleared of monks. After they were evicted the sacred images and books were destroyed or removed. Convoys of trucks shipped the valuables to China where gold and silver artifacts were melted into bullion. What remained of the population of Lhasa was organised for forced labour, obedience compelled by the grant of a small ration of food. The Panchen Lama was brought from China and installed as Acting Chairman of the Preparatory Committee of the Autonomous Region of Tibet.

The complete disruption of the country's political organisation, religious institutions and all normal life was now to be accompanied by a social revolution. The re-education of Tibet began.

. . . among them Tsarong who had stayed behind   The Panchen Lama was brought from China . . .

Chinese troops in front of the Potala

The new Tibet was to be hammered out on the anvil of communist ideology, the Class Struggle. The method was called Thamzing, meaning People's Courts, supervised by Chinese officials. Anyone who had had any kind of authority was publicly 'tried', denounced, abused, assaulted, tortured. Many died. The old hero, Tsarong, was one of the first to die. On the morning of May 14, 1959, the day he was to have faced a People's Court to be humiliated by his own servants, he was found dead on his mattress in his prison cell. Death had spared him the final injustice.

In the early sixties there was famine throughout China. With thousands of Tibetans rounded up and herded into labour camps, huge numbers died of starvation and exhaustion. The fabric of Tibet fell apart. Much of the food that was available went to feed the Chinese Army in Tibet.

The Panchen Lama's monastery, Tashilhunpo, was the only one, till then, to have remained unscathed. In late 1960, however, while the Panchen Lama was in Peking to give a report on the first year of progress in Tibet, the Chinese People's Liberation Army surrounded the great monastery and

Revolution Day Parade, Lhasa   182

evicted its 4,000 monks. Some of the incarnate lamas and abbots committed suicide, some were later shot; all the rest were deported to labour camps. The Panchen Lama was appalled. Two years later, with tremendous courage, he publicly denounced the Chinese occupation of Tibet and declared his support for the Dalai Lama. He was 'tried', assaulted and was last seen being driven out of Lhasa, with his parents and close followers, in a Chinese Army truck.

Refugees streamed across the Himalayas into India and Nepal. They were escaping what the International Commission of Jurists condemned as the systematic killing, imprisonment, torture and deportation of those Tibetans who opposed Chinese policies. India was not anxious to publicise the camps built to receive the refugees on the hot plains beneath the Himalayan foothills. The Chinese began to make threatening charges about India harbouring reactionaries. Nehru, the great believer in peaceful coexistence, was dismayed and concerned. There were outstanding differences between India and China about the border with Tibet.

In British times no country could have had a less aggressive neighbour. There had never been much need for access to India's northern border. Now,

183   'Friendship dancing', Lhasa, 1962

Tibetan refugees were found work constructing roads in the Himalayas. In 1962 Indian border posts on the frontier were overrun by the Chinese. It was for Nehru the final disillusionment with the idea of peaceful coexistence with China.

In India the Dalai Lama gratefully acknowledged the generous help that had been given to his people. More than 100,000 Tibetans had followed him into exile. In Dharmsala, a small hill-station in the mists of the Himalayan foothills, the Dalai Lama, with India's good will, had established a symbolic two-acre kingdom where the Tibetan religion and the spirit of the old Tibet were kept alive.

In the late sixties refugees were still crossing into India. The stories they told about what they had fled from were hard to believe. One old couple told how the Chinese had, 'destroyed our monasteries, burning temples and scattering the monks; they used the scriptures for stuffing mattresses and for putting in the road. They smashed all the gold and silver and other religious statues, and the clay statues were put in the lavatories. The stupas [Buddhist shrines] were pulled down. We saw the monks prevented from worshipping. An old lama and an old woman were forced to marry. In Tibet we have no freedom and have to do what the Chinese order.'

North of the Himalayas the most terrible chapter in Tibet's history had begun.

IT was 1967, the year of the Cultural Revolution in China. Hordes of doctrine-infatuated Red Guards descended on Lhasa determined to eradicate every vestige of the past. The great cathedral of Lhasa, the Jo-Khang, was ransacked. For several days it was filled with the smoke of burning scriptures as the mob rampaged, smashing images and defacing the ancient frescoes. Factions of Chinese fought in the streets and competed with each other in the destruction of everything Tibetan which was, by definition, reactionary. They destroyed the remaining monasteries, the libraries, the prayerflags, the shrines, the decorative borders to windows, house decorations, the distinctive Tibetan clothing. Women's long hair was cut off, pets were exterminated and pot plants smashed, in a preposterous outburst of violence. It is reported that female children were marched naked in public. Nomads were stripped and abused. Rapes and beatings turned into tortures and executions. Once again famine spread through the land.

The destruction was wholesale and calculated. Every building of religious or historical importance was desecrated; the ruins of some, like the great monastery of Ganden, were dynamited. Books and scriptures that were not

A country of ruins; of some three and a half thousand monasteries, temples and libraries, only parts of 13 are said to have survived intact. Top right is Ganden.

burnt were used as lavatory paper. Things of gold, silver or bronze were pulled down and shipped to China for smelting. It was an attempt at the extermination of an entire culture.

BY the middle of the 1970s the Cultural Revolution in Tibet was over, Chairman Mao dead. There was a new mood in China. The Chinese protested that they were innocent of the destruction of Tibet, that it was all the fault of the Gang of Four. The Panchen Lama was released from the prison where he had been held for 16 years.

Chairman Mao above the altar of the ancient Ramoche temple in Lhasa, photographed in 1983. Half of the ancient bronze statue it replaced was recently found in Peking, marked 'scrap metal'; the other half was found in a rubbish tip in Lhasa.

A 25-foot high pile of destroyed images and metalwork seen in a room in the Norbu-Lingka by the second delegation in 1980

The top of the derelict Ramoche temple, 1983

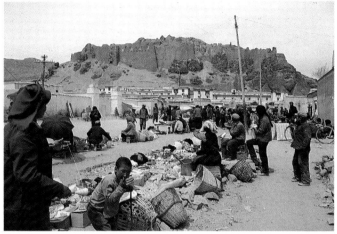

The Yambulakhang (photographed in 1936),
the first palace in Tibet, probably built
in the 7th century A.D. and completely demolished
by the Chinese, but now reconstructed

The ancient Dzong of Shigatse, totally destroyed

PLA soldiers posing beneath the Potala

Remaking images, 1983

Tibetans sifting broken pieces of images
from the rubble of the Jo-Khang, 1983

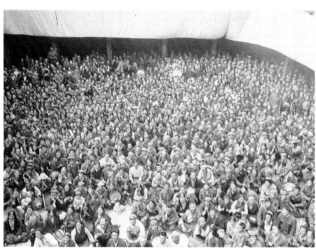

The continued exile of the Dalai Lama, however, was a constant reminder to the world that all was not well in Tibet. It was a source, too, of some embarrassment to the Chinese. The Dalai Lama was asked to consider returning to Tibet. They agreed that the Tibetans could send a delegation to investigate the situation in Tibet. It was over 20 years since the Chinese had occupied the country and forced the Dalai Lama to take refuge in India. The first delegation included two Tibetan Cabinet Ministers and the elder brother of the Dalai Lama. A second delegation, including Pema Gyalpo, the Dalai Lama's sister, followed shortly afterwards. Wherever they went they were besieged by thousands of excited Tibetans.

Born in eastern Tibet, Phuntsog Wangyal was admitted to the Drepung Monastery at the age of eight. He escaped into exile in India and now lives in London where till recently he was the Dalai Lama's representative. He went to Lhasa in 1980 as a member of the second delegation.

'Wherever we went people gathered in their thousands.'

'Exercises to Chinese music . . .'

'Thousands had gathered in the Jo-Khang.'

'Inscriptions used to build pavements . . .'

"WHEREVER we went people came in their thousands and thousands; even in eastern Tibet people gathered. They all wanted to ask about the Dalai Lama.

"It is not just the old people who have faith in the Dalai Lama and in religion, but even the younger people; they too came forward to see us, though it must have been the first time they had seen a lama. In all the time we were in Tibet we did not see more than three towns where there was a monastery; all had been destroyed. When we saw the state of their destruction and all the libraries pulled down we were really shocked. Sometimes they purposely placed religious objects where they should not be. For instance, the inscriptions had been used to build toilets and pavements, to insult religion.

"We had some 19 to 25 Chinese always with us and we said to them, 'Why do you do all these things?' I think they felt very embarrassed, because they never tried to defend themselves. They actually admitted to these destructions but always said, 'It is not our fault, it is the Gang of Four.'

"In the schools we visited we realised that what they teach is completely non-Tibetan, because, until 1979, no children could learn Tibetan. In textbooks they say, 'History of China, legend of Tibet.' All the clothes they wear are as in China; even the music they play over the loudspeakers is Chinese. You can hear it in Shanghai or Peking.

"Now, when you go to see people at work in the fields or constructing a building or road or canal, Tibetans are there; but when it comes to decisions you will see only Chinese. The decision-making and power rest with them.

"After two months travelling all over Tibet we came to Lhasa. In front of the Jo-Khang thousands of people had gathered and were shouting, 'Tibet is independent! Long live the Dalai Lama! May his wishes be fulfilled!' They broke down the railings and surrounded us. The Chinese could not say a word. They were astonished and thereafter some of the officials chose not come with us. They just left, they felt so embarrassed."

Many thousands of Tibetans mobbed the second delegation in Lhasa; so overwhelming was its reception by the people that the Chinese abruptly cancelled the tour. The delegation was flown back to Peking.

IT is unlikely that the Dalai Lama will return to Tibet in the near future. He believes that he can serve his people better from outside, keeping alive Tibetan culture and world concern for his country. He is a frequent traveller to Europe and America.

Today, in 1987, Lhasa is opening up to tourists drawn by the mysterious allure of Tibet. The Jo-Khang has been restored and visitors can wander through the Potala or the Norbu-Lingka unaware of how life was in Lhasa and of its sudden end. But few would want to know that it is not the same Tibet that for centuries so stirred men's curiosity.

Tibetans in exile are adaptable, resourceful people. They have spread throughout the world, to America and Britain, France, Switzerland and Germany. They are hard-working and generally successful, the most uncomplaining of refugees. They get on well with their host countries and many are sought after as teachers of religion and meditation. They maintain their culture and stimulate an interest in Tibet.

In exile they have symbolically recreated their great monasteries. The first monastery in Tibet, Samye, was founded in A.D.779. Much of it was destroyed by the Chinese. Today, keeping alive the name of Samye, a monastery has been re-established by Tibetans, at Eskdalemuir in Scotland. Barely 80 years ago no living European had seen Tibet. Now anyone may go to Samye and sit quietly in the temple before the image of Buddha. Tibet has come to the West.

SOURCES

This chapter is compiled from many sources: from Hugh Richardson's *Tibet and Its History*; from press cuttings and news reports; from Phuntsog Wangyal, for some years the Dalai Lama's representative in London; from Heinrich Harrer's *Return to Tibet* and from *Daughter of Tibet*, by Mary Taring, the wife of Jigme Taring. (The Tarings now live in Rajpur, in the foothills above Dehra Dun in North India.) The account of the destruction of Lhasa draws on John Avedon's book *In Exile From the Land of Snows*, a detailed account of the sufferings of Tibet after the Chinese invasion.

Samye, the first monastery in Tibet (photographed in 1936)

Samye in Scotland, 1987

His Holiness the Dalai Lama at the Albert Hall, on a recent visit to London. (Phuntsog Wangyal behind him)

POSTSCRIPT

I thought that I had finished this book but lorry-loads of Chinese troops are rattling once again through central Lhasa, tourists are being warned away, journalists expelled, monks rounded up and imprisoned. On October 1, 1987, the 37th anniversary of the Chinese invasion of Tibet, there was an anti-Chinese demonstration. Several thousand Tibetans demonstrated in the Barkhor, burnt down a police station, stoned the police and set fire to vehicles. Nineteen Tibetans and a number of Chinese police were killed.

It was a cry of despair to the world, despair of a subject people at the occupation of their country by alien, patronising foreigners from whom they are divided by a gulf of language, belief, nationality and culture.

There are today more Chinese in Tibet than Tibetans, three times as many in Lhasa. The Chinese have a colonial, imperial problem in Tibet but cannot comprehend why the Tibetans resent their presence so bitterly. Nationalism is long-lived and thrives on persecution. The Chinese angrily protest Tibet's past as feudal and exploitative, 'where people drank from human skulls, made drums from human skin'. This humiliating propaganda is contrary to the witness of those whose experiences are recorded in this book.

The outside world sees through this dismissive rhetoric, but the desire for a practical, working relationship with China conceals the inability to respect China for her treatment of Tibet. The Chinese cannot reject world concern by angrily saying it is interference with China's internal affairs; the abuse and degradation of a people concerns us all.

I have travelled much in China. I like the people and admire many aspects of their Revolution but in China the Revolution stemmed from the discontent of the ordinary people. In Tibet, it is above all the ordinary people who most resent the Chinese. One's earnest hope must be that wise council will prevail in Peking and some accommodation may be found that will allow the Tibetans to live as they wish, with their own peaceable religion and their Dalai Lama back in Lhasa. There should be no difference between China and Tibet that cannot be reconciled.